Finding Your Way In Troubled Times

Meditations for Modern Christians

MONSIGNOR
DENNIS CLARK

Cover: *Return of the Prodigal* by W. Ford Schumann, commissioned by
The Church of the Nativity.

Editors: Monsignor Loomis and Kathy Valyo

Consultant: Dan Farley

ISBN: 1499502966
ISBN 13: 9781499502961

FOREWARD

FINDING YOUR WAY IN TROUBLED TIMES is a product of lived experience, of years walking with people of all ages, faiths and circumstances in search of the deeper sense of purpose and peace that we all desire. It's a quest that takes on different shapes as our lives evolve sometimes gradually and sometimes with a jolt. None of us is exempt.

We can find ourselves overwhelmed by troubles we didn't cause and good fortune we didn't anticipate. We can awaken suddenly to a self we hardly know. And when we're most in need, we can find ourselves walking alone. This book is intended as a companion for such times - also for the in-between times of life. Whatever your circumstance, all that's required to find healing and light here is a listening heart.

Adult and teen prayer groups have found it helpful for systematic personal growth that these meditations are anchored in the Sunday gospels, as have busy pastors in search of homily inspiration. Opening anecdotes and parables provide easy entry points for people of all ages to reflection that draws them ever nearer to the Good that is our hearts' desire.

Whether for random dipping or as a daily or weekly companion for methodical spiritual growth, I hope that *FINDING YOUR WAY* will be a valued source of wisdom and spirit regeneration worthy of a place close at hand in your home.

TABLE OF CONTENTS

The respective cycles of readings and sermons begin with the First Sunday of Advent a month before the beginning of the calendar year. Thus, for example Cycle A for the church year 2014 actually begins in December 2013

Cycle A	Cycle B	Cycle C
2014	2015	2016
2017	2018	2019
2020	2021	2022
2023	2024	2025
2026	2027	2028
2029	2030	2031
2032	2033	2034

CYCLE A

GOD KNEW WE'D FORGET, SO HE GAVE US JESUS

There's a sad French film about a stranger who wanders into an empty village. There are signs of life all around: Food is on the table, smoke is curling up the chimneys, stores are open, but where are the people? The man doesn't know, and before long he's too drunk to notice that the villagers are all on a nearby hill, desperately trying to get his attention. They've fled because a bomb is about to go off in the town square.

They watch as he eats their food, drinks their wine, and tries on their clothes. But when he goes to the bank and starts flinging their money into the wind, it's too much. They *forget* about the bomb, rush back to town, beat up the stranger, and drive him out. At that moment, the bomb explodes and they all die - except the stranger!

✝

Forgetting can be dangerous, but we do it all the time. It's not just little things that we forget, our keys, a dental appointment, the causes of the Reformation, the cooking time for a rare steak. We forget the big things as well: how good it is to be alive, how right it is to share what we have, and how blessed we are to have so many people who love us. And worst of all, we forget how to live so that we won't be afraid to die.

Forgetting so much of what truly matters leaves the world painted in shades of gray and blinds us to life's real joys. And it leaves us easy prey to bitterness and despair. We stop welcoming the new day and the new friend and instead retreat into ourselves, closing the doors behind us.

It's a slow form of suicide, and that's why Jesus calls out to us, "Wake up! Remember who you are and why our Father made you - not for a sad, slow drift into nothingness, but for a real life in the embrace of his big family!"

God knew we'd forget sometimes, so he sent Jesus to walk with us and to help us remember. No matter what your age, happiness is within your reach - if only you stay close to him and let him help you remember always what a blessed gift every day of life truly is.

Stay close to him and despair will never find a place in your heart!

JUST WAITING WON'T MAKE THE KINGDOM COME!

Waiting is one of our least favorite pastimes, but there's no escaping it. The little waits: for the gas tank to fill, the stop light to change, or the water to boil. We can't do much about them.

The longer waits: for second grade to be over, our cold to run its course, or our tax refund to come. We can't do much about them either.

And the still longer waits: for the last child to graduate, for the last day of work, for the grandchildren to finally get baptized. The most we can say is it'll happen when it happens.

So much of life is beyond our control that we're easily blinded to what we *can* control and change. When we hear the amazing promises in the scriptures - a new shoot growing from a dead stump, a lamb having lunch with a lion and not being lunch - our first reaction is: I surely hope it happens, but it's beyond me.

That reaction is dead wrong, for in giving us Jesus, God planted the seeds of the just and peaceful world we long for. And generation by generation, he puts in our hands the time and the talent to make those seeds grow. They *will* grow, the kingdom *will* come, as the Lord's Prayer says, if we let Jesus guide us.

The place to start is within, where the wolves and lions and cobras live. For there can be no peace or justice *among* us, if there is no peace *within* us. If wants and desires, fears and dreads, angers and envies rule our hearts, God's kingdom can never come to this place. If hand-wringing helplessness defines our relation to the world, God's kingdom will permanently evade our grasp.

†

Take hold of your gifts. Take to heart everything Jesus has shown you about what a good life is and what it's not. Begin to make peace within your own soul and then with the world. It's slow work, but it will bear fruit if you persist.

DO YOU LOVE YOURSELF
AS GOD LOVES YOU?

A young man was walking along a beach when he came upon a lantern half buried in the sand. He rubbed it vigorously, and of course, a genie popped out and offered him anything he wanted! The young man wanted a gift that would keep on giving, so he asked for the Midas touch. And that's exactly what he got. For the rest of his life, everything he touched turned into a muffler!

✝

False expectations mean trouble, as John the Baptist learned to his sorrow. His interpretation of Isaiah's prophecies had led him to expect a swift turnaround of this sinful world as soon as the Messiah came: deserts would bloom, the weak would be strong, and virtue would reign. The reality was different: Jesus came, but nothing changed. John felt betrayed, so he sent messengers with a pointed question: "Are you the promised one, or must we keep waiting?"

Failed expectations can be especially troubling when they involve our own performance. We want to succeed, to please our parents and the Lord, and *never* to sin. But in real life, our days are confusing *mixtures* of success and failure. We anguish over our mistakes and devalue our achievements. And all too easily, our sadness hardens into self-disgust and despair. So how do we break out of this trap so many of us make for ourselves? I think Jesus might tell us three things:

1. Don't expect perfection this side of the grave.

2. Invest your whole self in each day - and when it's done, let it go and give it to God.

3. And remember the unspoken middle line of the Golden Rule: *Love yourself as God loves you.* (If you despise yourself, your neighbor hasn't got a chance!)

You're still going to fall short and make foolish mistakes. But you won't lose hope, because you know that the Father who gave you life loves you even more than you love yourself.

✝

Love *God* with all your heart.

Love yourself as *God* loves you.

And then, love your neighbor as you love yourself.

STEP INTO THE DARKNESS

A man went to his doctor, very upset about his health. "What's your problem?" asked the doctor.

"When I look in the mirror, I see sagging jowls, thinning hair, and bloodshot eyes. What's happening to me?"

"I really don't know," said the doctor. "But the good news is: Your eyesight is perfect."

✝

Reality doesn't always match our hopes and dreams.

St Joseph had dreamed a long time about the wonderful family he was going to have with Mary: lots of children and later on, grandchildren. Even the thought of it warmed his heart. And then, in a trice, it was gone. Mary was pregnant and he wasn't the father. The door to all his hopes slammed shut in his face.

But God opened another door. What lay beyond it was still invisible, but Joseph trusted God so thoroughly that he walked through that door anyway. There was no houseful of children on the other side, and not a single grandchild, but there *was* Jesus. It was more than Joseph could ever have hoped for. But none of it would have happened if he'd said "no" to God and refused to take that step into the dark unknown.

All too often, life confounds our hopes and expectations. Doors slam shut without warning. Our hopes wilt. All we can see is fog and darkness. We're left with only one real choice: embrace the present. Walk *into* it, one step at a time, confident that God will help us to see what he sees and to find the good that's hidden there.

The psalm tells us, "Be stout-hearted and wait for the Lord." It's good advice, because in his own good time, the Lord will show himself, and what has been hidden will be made clear. Trust that, and your soul will be at peace, even now!

Christmas
Luke 2: 1-14

JESUS'S COMING IS GOD'S PROMISE OF LIFE

Once upon a stormy Christmas Eve, as the winds howled and the snows swirled, a family sat drowsily by their cozy fire, waiting for the hour of Midnight Mass. Suddenly, they were roused by two loud thumps at the window: two little birds, driven by the winds and confused by the snow, had flown straight into the glass.

They would surely die if left in the freezing cold. So the man grabbed his coat and plunged out into the storm to see if couldn't bring them inside. But the birds, fluttered out of his reach again and again. In frustration, the man returned to his kitchen. He cut a loaf of bread into crumbs and made a tiny trail of crumbs out to the birds, hoping to lure them into the warmth and safety of his house. But they'd have nothing to do with him. Their fears kept them hiding at a distance in the cold and the darkness.

With a heavy heart, he said to his wife, "If only I could become one of them, I could show them they have no reason to be afraid, no reason to stay out in the cold and die there. I could lead them in where it's warm and safe." No sooner had he said this than he knew why Jesus came.

We celebrate Christmas because we know that Jesus' is God's solemn promise that we have no reason to be afraid, no reason to languish in the dark and to die in the cold. For we have a God who is with us always, and who is, at this very moment, calling us out of the darkness and into the light and warmth and joy of His presence.

†

Answer his call, welcome his coming, and make haste into his embrace!

Holy Family - A
Matthew 2:13-15, 19-23

LIVE THE TRUTH IN LOVE AND FAMILY WILL SURELY FOLLOW

Grandpa was invited to supper and was left with his little grandson in the living room.

"Well, Billy," said grandpa, "What are we going to have for supper?"

"Goat!" replied Billy.

"Goat?! What makes you say that?"

"I heard Mama tell Daddy this morning: 'Remember, George, we're having the old goat for supper tonight.'"

†

Families are complex and confusing places. The Holy Family was no exception: Mary was totally confused and frightened by the angel's startling news; Joseph was brokenhearted and thought he'd have to divorce her; and as time passed the two of them were amazed and confused as they watched their little boy grow up. Finding him in the temple after a three-day search was just the latest of an endless string of perplexing events.

The three of them, Jesus, Mary and Joseph, were all persons of world-class goodness, but they had to work hard to understand each other and to know how to respond to each other as day followed day and year followed year. As it was for them, so it is for us.

Every one of us is a mystery - even to ourselves. And that makes it all the more difficult to know how to respond to one another. It's something we have to learn, mostly by trial and error, and family is where we have to learn it.

A family is a "conversation" in word and deed that proceeds, across many decades. If that conversation is ever to create understanding hearts, we have to step *outside* ourselves and *into* our neighbors' lives and see everything our merciful God sees there. And then our gaze must turn inward again, to look with God at the rooms full of ancient hopes, failures, memories and plans, silent fears and secret betrayals that lie hidden within us. We must own them all.

Jesus didn't stand outside people's lives and throw stones; he entered their hearts and felt their wounds and their sadness. He showed us the proper work of family: understanding, forgiving, helping and saving. Young or old, that's *our* work.

✝

How is your family doing on its great work? Are *you* doing *your* part by building an understanding heart? You are if you've learned to *speak the truth in love* - first to yourself and then to you neighbor - and then *to live the truth in love*. Do it now, even if you're very old. Live the truth in love, and true family will slowly follow!

THEY KNEW SOMETHING WAS MISSING

There's a new technology that's become quite common in automobiles: the Global Positioning System. With the help of a satellite connection, it knows exactly where your car *is* at any given moment, and it can tell you exactly how to get where you *want* to go next. It's a clever gadget, but even with all its powers, it can't tell us where we really *need* to go. That's something we have to figure out on our own, and it's no easy matter.

†

There's a longing deep inside us. It has no name and no face, but it keeps us restless and vaguely dissatisfied even when our lives are filled with good things. Many people ignore that feeling and just keep going after more of what they already have. It doesn't work; you can see it in their faces.

The Wise Men in the Christmas story weren't like that. They knew something essential was missing from their lives. So they probed deeper and deeper into themselves and into the hearts of their neighbors. They read and studied and talked among themselves long into the night. And finally there was a glimmer of light. They weren't sure what it meant, but they pursued it, and it led to places they'd never been before. It even brought them into the presence of the evil King Herod, who didn't understand their quest, because he'd never looked inside himself or beyond himself. Thus he never saw the star.

When at last the Wise Men found their way to the stable, the painful emptiness within them was full, and life made sense once and for all. They'd come face to face with God, they knew they were loved with an undying love, and they knew at last what their lives were for: returning God's love by loving and caring for God's people.

✝

So it was that the best part of their life's journey began.

And so may it be for you!

HAVE YOU LEARNED TO READ THE SIGNS OF THE TIMES?

A young priest was in his car when he saw two people lying face down on a lawn. He was curious, so he pulled over and asked what they were doing. The man said they were homeless and were eating grass because they didn't have anything else.

"You can eat over at the church," said the priest.

"We have nine children," warned the woman. "Will there be enough?"

"Oh sure," said the priest. "The grass is much taller over there!"

✝

Getting a solid grip on our life's work is never easy. Jesus himself had to struggle and pray a long time before he could see his mission clearly. But when he saw it, he asked John to baptize him. It had nothing to do with being washed clean; Jesus had no sins. He was putting himself shoulder-to-shoulder with all of us sinners, who *do* need to be washed clean. He was holding out his hand to everyone who'd ever get lost in the dark.

Because Jesus listened to the Spirit deep within and kept no part of his life off limits, he became profoundly wise and compassionate, able to heal and forgive, and ready to face whatever might come.

That's where we'd all like to end up: knowing where God wants us to go and being willing to do whatever it takes to get there. The key is to watch the "signs of the times," watch where God's gifts are pointing us. But that's not so easy, because the world keeps changing, and so do we. So there *is* no permanent answer to the question: what does God want of me? Just today's answer. We'll have to listen again tomorrow.

†

Watch and listen with an open heart; as Jesus did, keep saying "yes;" keep pushing the limits of your imagination and your courage further and further out. As you give the Spirit more and more room, what the Spirit can accomplish *in* and *through* you will increase every day, until at last there'll be no limits on the Spirit at all.

Ordinary 2 - A
John 1:24-39

ARE YOU MISSING THE BEST
PARTS OF LIFE?

The village drunk was staggering along Main Street when he saw a priest and asked him, "Father, could you tell me what causes arthritis?"

Father tried to ignore him, but finally snapped: "Drinking causes arthritis, and so does gambling and carousing. Why do you ask?"

"Because it says in the paper, that's what the pope has!"

✝

Father might have seen that coming, if he hadn't been caught up in his own thoughts.

Failing to see what we could and should see is a common experience, often with dire consequences. John the Baptist had known his cousin Jesus since birth, and he thought he knew him inside out. But he didn't, as he admitted with acute embarrassment: "I confess I didn't recognize him!" How could that happen to someone as smart and single-minded as John? Easily. He was so focused on his work and so blinded by what he assumed about Jesus, that he never looked any deeper.

It happens to us all. To avoid drowning in the sea of data that pours into our heads every day, we *have* to filter out what we don't need. And it's inevitable that sometimes we'll filter out what we *do* need: just think "investments 2007"! Even in our spiritual lives, there are crucial areas where our filters get overloaded and leave us with a blank screen:

- First of all, we miss most of the abundant hints of God's presence: the miracles of nature, the astonishing goodness of ordinary people, the subtle nudges of the Spirit within. They get filtered out as we struggle to avoid a crash on a rainy freeway or search for the right words for a letter that needed to go out yesterday. And we're left with painful doubts and a life painted in shades of gray.

- And then there's the life-giving face and voice of Jesus, which should be our abiding comfort and strength. But amidst the swirl of the necessary business of life, we let Him drift out of our consciousness. Without meaning to, we let go of His hand and falter as we try to walk alone.

- Finally there's the courage and decency of our own lives, which should give us confidence as we face new challenges. But it gets screened out by our demanding schedule and the paralyzing memory of past mistakes. And we feel powerless as we look into the future.

- How do we break this pattern of missing the best parts of life? We make our filters work for us instead of against us. We take hold of moments throughout the day, filter out the busyness for just a little while, and let the goodness of life and the tender presence of the Lord wrap us round.

✝

Stop walking alone. Use those powerful filters of yours to create special moments with Him every day. Take his hand, and let him remind you how good it is to be alive. And then smile and give thanks!

THE LIFELONG JOURNEY FROM SELF-ABSORPTION TO SELF-TRANSCENDENCE

A patient in a psychiatric ward was convinced that he was a corpse, and nothing his doctors could say would dissuade him. He was willing to agree that corpses don't bleed, so his doctors persuaded him to submit to a simple test: they pricked his finger and, of course, a drop of blood come forth. The patient looked at the blood for quite a while, and then said, "Well I'll be darned, corpses *do* bleed!"

✝

Real changes of mind and heart come hard. But they're not optional if we want to reach wholeness, where all the parts of our life are integrated by love and *everything fits*. A person who is whole can't go to church on Sunday and then cheat on Monday. The two just don't fit.

Building this kind of integrity is a tall order. We have to deal with the accumulated *residue* of our personal history: longstanding resentments, debilitating fears, compulsive acquisitiveness, habitual shortcuts around truth, and more. And because each of us is in a lifelong process of *evolution*, we have to keep sorting out what needs to be let go and what needs to take its place as we reach a new stage of life.

For example, at age five, the child is learning to take care of *my* toys, which, of course, his *parents gave* him. At 35, he's scrambling to get stuff to *provide for himself* and his family. And at 65, he's *giving* himself and his stuff away without expecting anything in return. That's just a peek at the repeated shifts of mind and heart that our evolution toward wholeness and freedom requires.

✝

Whatever your stage in life, don't duck the question. Open your soul to the Lord. Let him help you probe the darkness and reach for truth. Give it serious time: *this is your life!* And pray often: "Lord, there's nothing that you and I can't handle together."

WHAT DEFINES WHO YOU ARE?

Every year catastrophic floods occur here and there around the world.

Homes, offices and farms are buried beneath the waters, and with them the hopes and dreams of countless good people. Their familiar haunts are hidden from sight. They know that grandma's clock is ruined and their keepsakes and pictures are reduced to mush. It feels as if their lives have been erased, and they begin to wonder who they are, and before long they begin to find out.

✝

When we're asked to tell who we *are,* most of us tell what we *do* - that's just how we think about ourselves: she's a litigator, he's a developer, I'm a writer. And we likely add where we live and other hints of our accomplishments: my son the doctor, our new home, my new book.

But that happy picture can disappear in a trice: a child dies, a fortune is lost, a home is burned to the ground, old age does its worst. If our lifestyle and achievements are what we've used to define ourselves, there won't be much left of us when they're taken away or cease to count - just our empty skins and a future of sadness.

In the eight beatitudes, sometimes called the eight congratulations, Jesus gives us a very different starting point for thinking about who we *are.*

"Blessed are the poor in spirit," he says. Or, a better yet, *"Congratulations* to those who *know* they are poor!"

Knowing we're poor is the base line for an honest life: we own nothing. It's all gift from God, who made us simply because His goodness can't be contained. Yet, as poor as we are, we're priceless, because He made us like himself: we can love! And the core of our life's work is to build a great heart. That's the real source of our identity: something so powerfully good that neither flood nor fire nor even death can destroy.

Building such a heart starts with soul-filling gratitude that runs deep and impels us:

- — to live graciously and walk gently upon the earth,

- — to step outside ourselves and do whatever love requires, and

- — to trust always that the Lord loves us even when we don't much love ourselves.

†

Walk that long road with the Lord. Your heart will grow spacious and ready for whatever may come. Joy will be yours even to your last day and thence to eternity.

MANY ARE WAITING FOR YOUR SALT AND YOUR LIGHT!

Little Jethro and his family were visiting the big city for the first time. In the lobby of their fancy hotel, he and his pa were fascinated by the elevator. "What in tarnation is that?" asked Jethro.

"I don't rightly know," said Pa as an old woman stepped into the elevator and the doors closed. When doors reopened moments later, out stepped a gorgeous young blonde!

Pa immediately saw the possibilities: "Son, go get your ma!"

✝

There's a lot that needs to be made new in this old world of ours. And sometimes we wish we had a pair of those shiny elevator doors that would just set things right. But we don't. So we shuffle on, sad at much of what we see and feeling powerless to change it.

But Jesus saw more in us than we do. He didn't say, "you *should be* the light of the world and the salt of the earth." He said, "you *are* the light...and the salt..." We *have* in us the power to make life better. Jesus could see it!

Salt brings out the best in things; and as a preservative it prevents things from going bad. To *be* salt for people means bringing out the best in them and pulling them back when they're about to sleepwalk over a cliff. We *are* salt, if we choose to be.

Light reveals the world - both within and without. To *be* light for people means helping them to see reality and wrestle with it and to see where life's real joys are - and where they're not. We *are* light, if we choose to be.

But to *be* salt and light for one another takes wisdom which can see that:

— there are many good roads to most goals, and we mustn't impose ours,

— growth comes slowly, and we must be willing to wait, and

— the Spirit will guide us, if we let ourselves be guided.

✝

Many people are waiting for *your* salt and *your* light. So don't let your salt lose its savor or your light grow dim. Let the Lord feed your soul and refresh your love, and you'll never disappoint.

Ordinary 6 - A
Sirach 15:15-20 & Matthew 5:17-37

RULE-KEEPING DOESN'T WORK IF YOUR HEART'S NOT IN IT

President Lincoln was talking with one of his generals: "See that dog over there. How many legs does it have?"

"Four," said the general.

"But if we called his tail a leg, how many legs would it have then?"

"Five, of course," replied the general.

"No," said Lincoln. "Whatever we may choose to *call* its tail, that dog still has only four legs!"

✝

And so it is with the core of our life. *Calling* ourselves Christians doesn't make it so, anymore than sitting in our garage makes us a Mercedes.

Jesus said, "whoever breaks *one* of the *least* of the commandments will be *least* in the kingdom of God." So it seems that if we want heaven, we'd better be superior rule keepers. But perhaps not. For on another occasion Jesus showed us a classic rule-keeping pharisee, and called him a failure in the eyes of God. So what *is* Jesus telling us?

The rules that really count were written on our hearts by God, long before Moses put them on tablets of clay: don't lie, cheat or steal, worship God and him alone. They aren't optional, and we'll destroy ourselves if we ignore them. But they're useless, if we treat them as nothing more than fire insurance, a cynical deal with God to avoid hell. There's no life in that!

And just as dangerous is our readiness to trivialize. In no time at all, worshiping God morphes into lighting candles to pay off St Jude for services rendered. The no-stealing rule morphes into nothing more than avoiding armed robberies. And the no-adultery rule morphes into debating what the meaning of "is" is.

Rule-keeping doesn't work if our heart isn't in it! The commandments are an invitation to invest ourselves in a big-hearted life with God and his people. They're a starting line, not the finish line. Jesus *said:* "Love God with *all* your heart, *all* your soul, and *all* your mind, and your neighbor as yourself."

And that's what he *did!* He gave himself wholeheartedly into every moment, doing whatever was needed, and never counting the cost, just loving us and hoping we'd get it. It brought him to the cross, but even then he didn't turn away.

†

Keep your eyes and your heart fixed on Jesus. He'll show you the way, and he'll give you the courage to walk it.

LET GOD HELP YOU BE RECONCILED

Little Ben desperately wanted a baby sister, so he wrote a letter: "Dear God, I've been a very good boy..." He stopped: "No, God won't believe that." So he started over: "Dear God, most of the time I've been a good boy..." He stopped again: "That won't work either."

Then suddenly Ben knew what he had to do. He grabbed a large bath towel and spread it out on the living room floor. Next he took the statue of the Virgin Mary down from the mantle, wrapped it in the towel and hid it deep in the linen closet. Then he returned to his desk: "Dear God, if you ever want to see your mother again..."

✝

Ben's ethics were a little dicey, but he knew how to think big. And that's what Jesus is challenging us to do when people do us wrong. The popular wisdom is "don't get mad, get even." But that doesn't work. It just poisons life and prolongs our hurt.

Jesus gave us an alternative: "Love your enemies and pray for your persecutors." Our first reaction is "sounds great, but no can do!" To which Jesus replies, "Yes, you can." And then he reminds us of a bit of reality that should soften our hearts: "God makes his sun shine on both the just *and* the unjust, and lets his rain fall on both the good *and* the bad." Who *are* these "good" and "bad", "just" and "unjust" people? We're both every day.

Yet this morning every one of us received the gift of another day, despite anything wrong we may have done yesterday. God doesn't waste time getting even. He looks deep into our hearts, and there he sees our struggles and feels our hurts. And from deep in his heart he says, "I understand. Let me help you."

✝

Let him help *you*. Let his love soften your heart. Then look again at the person who's been driving you crazy, and the one who's cheated you, and the one who gossiped about you. And keep looking until you see what God sees, a confused human being who's struggling to make a life and who needs help - just as you do.

And then do what God has been doing for you all your life long: understand and forgive!

NO ONE CAN SERVE TWO MASTERS

Little Eddie was thrilled to get the part of the angel in the Christmas play. In the final scene, he'd proclaim: "Glory to God in the highest, and peace on earth to men of good will!"

So when the great moment came, Eddie was dropped into view with garments flowing and wings flapping, and he began to speak the ancient words: "Glory to God and...and..." He couldn't remember. So he tried again, "Glory to God and...and...I'll huff and I'll puff and I'll blow your house down!"

✝

Poor Eddie got lost somewhere between the gospel and the three little pigs. It's a very human problem: getting lost between two sets of values. And it always means trouble, for "no one can serve two masters."

Yet we keep trying. Some of us lack focus and just don't notice that the pieces of our life don't fit. Some of us fear that really following Jesus would mean missing out on life's "gusto." And some of us doubt that God even exists, but hedge our bets by going to church once in awhile.

We all have our doubts, fears and confusions, which cloud our vision and fragment our lives. So we need to listen to Jesus, who could see God at work all around him: "Look at the birds of the sky," he said. "They neither sow nor reap, they gather nothing into barns; yet your heavenly Father feeds them. Aren't you more important than a whole flock of sparrows?"

Indeed we are! But what exactly does that mean? God isn't promising to shield us from disappointment, pain, or death. He isn't absolving us from the hard work of planning and building a decent future. But he *is* promising us the power to face whatever comes and to take the boulders that fall in our path and convert them to stepping stones. He can give us that power, if we listen to him - and walk with him.

At times, of course, darkness will fall upon us, and we'll feel alone and forgotten. That's when we need to remember what the Lord said to Isaiah at just such a moment: "Can a mother forget her infant, or be without tenderness for her child? Even should she forget, I will never forget you."

✝

Trust his love. He's closer to you than you are to yourself!

Lent 1 - A
Matthew 4:1-11

DON'T LET THE CONVERSATION DIE

Three old buddies arrived at the gates of heaven, where St Peter asked them a simple question: "What is Easter?"

"That's easy," said the first. "It's when we give thanks and eat turkey." A trapdoor opened and he was gone.

The second man said, "It's when we get a tree, give presents, and celebrate the birth of Jesus." The trapdoor opened again.

The third was smug. "Easter is the Christian feast that coincides with Passover. Jesus was betrayed by Judas, crucified by the Romans, and buried in a cave sealed by a boulder." Peter was beaming, but then the guy went on: "Every year the boulder is moved aside so Jesus can come out, and if he sees his shadow, there'll be six more weeks of winter."

✝

Something was missing there!

Too often we've watched arrogant players on the international stage destroy themselves and countless others, and we've wondered why. Something seems to be missing at their center, a crucial fabric that should have been woven across a lifetime. But it isn't there. So when their decisive moment came, they had no inner safety net, nothing to catch them and break their fall, so they crashed and burned.

Before he began his ministry, Jesus faced his own decisive moment: who would he be for the rest of his life? The savior of us all or just another power-hungry madman? He was *free* to choose. But in fact his decision was long since made, because a lifetime of conversation with the Spirit had formed in him a soul so strong and true that not even death could turn him aside.

We all have our own decisive moments to face - often more than one. Will we stand tall and true, or will we betray God's gift of life? It all depends on our ongoing conversation with the Spirit. If it's nothing more than a rerun of old tapes, we're starving our souls and we're headed for trouble.

A real conversation with the Spirit means listening, letting the Spirit's light shine into every corner of our life - and then facing whatever we find. It means seeing our gifts and accepting the challenge to use them. And in the end, it means learning how to love with *all* our hearts.

✝

Your soul is the "who-you-are" which you'll take into eternity. Don't starve your soul. Don't lose your self. Walk with the Spirit, listen, and live.

WALK THROUGH THE NEW DOOR AND DON'T LOOK BACK

A young man from a wealthy family was being divorced by his glamorous wife. His lawyer called him about the property settlement: "The good news is that she isn't asking for any share of your future inheritance."

"Great!" said the young man. "What's the bad news?"

"After the divorce, she's marrying your father!"

✝

Abraham must have had that same sinking feeling when God told him - at age 75! - to pack up his family, gather his flocks, and leave the only home he'd ever known. "I'm going to take you to a wonderful new place," said the Lord, "but I'm not going to tell you where it is." It was an intriguing promise; but not knowing where he was going was profoundly unsettling!

Life is like that. Time and again we find ourselves in circumstances we haven't faced before - and with no map and no owner's manual. We say to ourselves: but I haven't been a first grader before or a college freshman before. I haven't been married or a priest or the pope before. I haven't been unemployed or old or had a heart attack before.

At every new stage of life, a familiar door closes and a new one opens, though it often takes us a while to find that door. When we do, will we dare to walk through it? Will we figure out how to take what we find there and make a new life? Or will we waste months and years trying to get back into rooms that are now locked to us forever?

It all depends on who's with us when a new door opens. If we're walking alone, it will probably be more than we can handle, and we'll just cave in upon ourselves. But if we've been walking with the Lord all along, a new door may make us nervous, but it won't break us. We'll begin to see that this new place has something we needed to complete our journey, but hadn't realized it yet. And with a trusting heart, we'll step forward.

✝

Step forward with confidence when the next segment of your journey reveals itself. And don't look back. The Lord is with you *here and now*. And he'll *stay* with you all the way home.

Lent 3 - A
John 4:5-42

IS THIS ALL THERE IS?

Some sight-seers drove into a dusty little town in the west Texas. It was hard-shell Baptist country: no drinkin' and no dancin'! But they were thirsty, so they asked a cowboy if there were any way they could get a drink.

"In this town," he said, "we only use whiskey for snakebite." Then he added slyly, "There's only one snake in town, so you better get in line before it gets worn out!"

✝

The woman who came upon Jesus as he rested by a well had a mighty thirst, so deep that it had led her through five husbands and who knows what else. And still her soul was dry and full of longing, though she couldn't quite say what she was looking for. But Jesus knew. So he set aside his travel weariness and gently probed her heart with a kindness and patience she'd never known before. She discovered face to face what God's love is like: it's whisper is quiet and gently respectful, but it has the power to give life and hope. Her heart caught fire, and she rushed to tell her friends what she'd found.

Like that woman, we have a mighty thirst. Across the years, we've made decent lives for ourselves, and we have ample reason to be pleased. But still there's a restlessness in us, a sense that something important is missing.

And we remember Peggy Lee's song from the '60s: *Is This All There Is?* There's a God-shaped hole in our souls, waiting to be filled. St Augustine said it well: "Our hearts are restless, Lord, until they rest in you."

That uneasy and often painful sense of something missing, even in the midst of comfortable lives, is a gift from God. He's inviting us to look at the world more closely, to see the imprint of his presence all around us - and deep within us, and to embrace his presence and let him fill that deep hole in our souls.

✝

The Lord is calling you from deep within. Answer him as the prophet Samuel did so long ago: "Speak, Lord, your servant is listening." Let him wrap you round with his love and fill you with his peace.

ARE YOU LIVING IN A SPIRITUAL POOR HOUSE?

A Russian team faced the Americans in an international boat race, and the Americans won by a mile. Moscow was furious, but they saw the problem: the Americans had one manager and seven rowers, while they had seven managers and only one rower! So they sent in a new team, seven senior bureaucrats and one rower, and lost by two miles! By now Moscow was desperate, so they acted decisively...and fired the rower!

†

It's astonishing how blind we can be. We overlook our gifts. We don't notice that we're loved. And we don't see how to get better, because we're not good at looking inward. So we shuffle along on the surface of things, living in a spiritual poorhouse and clinging to vague hopes that will never come true.

Why are we so blind? Sometimes it's *habit and inertia*. We see what we expect to see. (That's what makes proofreading so challenging!) We don't look, because we think we already know the answers.

Sometimes *fear* keeps us blind. We don't look at what's wrong, because we're afraid we can't change it. That's why battered women stick around and tell themselves: "It's not so bad."

Sometimes it's *cultural values* that keep us blind. Our culture tells us it's foolish to spend time every day looking inward and remembering what matters. Sound bites are enough! So we stay busy and blind and wonder why life doesn't get any better.

But that's not how our story *has* to end. Again and again Jesus reached out to a people who were born blind and helped them to see, not just the world around them, but the world within - the world of the spirit. And with that, a new kind of life, a conscious life, was within their reach.

These weren't unique events, for the Lord is extending his hand to every one of us, calling us out of the blindness we've made for ourselves. "Don't be afraid," he says, and don't give in to inertia. Open your eyes. Get to know your real self, and never doubt that you're loved and forgiven. Get to know your neighbors, not just your image of them, and see how good they are and how much they need you.

Love the truth, and live it. And always give thanks that you're not walking alone.

LAY CLAIM TO THE TRUTH THAT CAN SET YOU FREE

The sole survivor of a shipwreck was washed ashore on a remote island. He prayed for rescue, but no one came. So he built a little hut as shelter from the fierce storms. But then a lightning strike burned the hut to the ground and left him with nothing at all.

"God, how could you do this to me?" he cried, throwing himself on the beach in despair. But next morning, he was awakened by the voices of sailors coming to his rescue. "How did you know I was here?" he asked.

The sailors replied: "We saw your smoke signal!"

✝

Even the best of us needs rescuing at times, whether we know it or not. We're remarkably adept at getting ourselves in trouble. We let hurts and hates take hold of us. We get trapped in other people's expectations and in cravings for things we don't need. And the more we get caught in those traps, the harder it is to remember who we are and how to make a life that *is* a life.

It's been said that the majority of people die before the age of thirty, but just don't get buried for another 50 years. The body keeps going, but the heart is gone. It's a frightening thought! So we need to remember Jesus standing at his friend's tomb and calling him: "Lazarus, come out!" He was calling *us* as well. And when he said, "Untie him and set him free!" he was offering *us* freedom too. We don't *have* to be dead men walking. We have an alternative!

It begins with recognizing the traps we've wandered into so blindly. That isn't easy. It may take a tragedy like a death or a fire, or a devastating public embarrassment, or if we're lucky, just a candid word from a trusted friend. But however our self-recognition begins, we have to lay claim to the truth and make it our own: "Lord, I've fallen into something that has no life in it. And I can't break free unless you help me."

That humble truth-telling is the key to life on a new level. It opens our soul to a real partnership with the Lord, and it brings a new intensity to our desire to walk with Him always.

✝

Take the Lord's hand, speak the truth that needs to be spoken, and step with Him into a new future.

ARE YOU WORTH DYING FOR? JESUS THOUGHT SO!

The juxtaposition of the two gospels of Palm and Passion Sunday underscores with brutal clarity a stunning reversal: Jesus was acclaimed as a hero and then executed as a heretic - all within hours. The thoughtless ease with which the crowd turned on him raises a stark question: were they really worth dying for? Why didn't Jesus just make a swift about-face and go home to a happy life with his family?

The question becomes even more poignant when we look at the cynicism and fecklessness of our own day - and even of our own lives. Are *we* worth dying for? Though it may be hard to see why, Jesus thought we are. For he could see in us a faint yet real reflection of the goodness of God - a goodness that could grow. And none of the thoughtlessness and narcissism of his generation - or of ours - could deter him from pouring his whole self into giving us a chance at a real life.

How could he bring himself to do that? It's truly a mystery which only those who love deeply will ever begin to understand. We can only give thanks and let our gratitude flower into love that lasts.

LISTEN TO THOSE WHISPERS
IN YOUR SOUL

A little boy and his grandpa were on a hill flying a kite. It soared higher and higher until finally a cloud hid it from sight. "Bobby," said grandpa, "do you think maybe a robber up there stole your kite?"

"No, grandpa!" said the boy.

A little later, grandpa said, "I'll *bet* some robber up in that cloud *did* steal your kite."

But the boy's answer was still "no."

Finally grandpa asked, "Bobby, why are you so *sure* you've still got a kite up there?"

The boy replied, "Because I can *feel* the kite tugging at my string."

†

All our lives *we've* felt little tugs at our heart and quiet whispers in our soul, telling us there's more to life than we can see - something beyond our imagining, just over the horizon of our minds. Most of the time those inner tugs are so quiet that we barely notice them, but they've always been there.

Jesus talked to us about those whispers in our soul. He told us we can trust them, because they're from God, who wants us to know that we're his very dear children and not mere throwaways. We *want* to believe Jesus, but it isn't easy when life's hurts and losses - and death itself - seem to say just the opposite. We're afraid of being fooled by pretty words and our own wishful thinking.

So Jesus gave us something we could count on. He willingly *gave* us his own dying and being buried in a cold tomb, and then rising from the dead as the guarantee that the tugs we've always felt in our hearts *can* be trusted. God didn't make us just to suffer and weep - and then to die. He made us for eternal life in his very own embrace!

✝

Trust the Good News that's always been there tugging at your heart: Jesus our brother is risen from the dead! And when your journey is done, *you* will rise with Him!

BE STOUTHEARTED AND
WAIT FOR THE LORD

An old couple was being interviewed on their 70th anniversary, and the interviewer asked how they'd done it. The old fellow replied, "The 70 years felt like seven minutes," and then added softly, "under water."

†

We all have our troubles, and some of them last a long time. But it's what we *do* with our troubles that makes us who we are - heroes or empty shells. The apostle Thomas is a good example. Like all the apostles, he'd been devastated by Jesus' brutal crucifixion. He hadn't seen it coming, and when it did, it broke his heart.

It was a crucial turning point, but which way would he turn? Would he act impulsively and run away, or would he wait until he could see where God was calling him? Thomas quieted his soul and waited. He returned to the upper room, and there he got the surprise of his life: Jesus was alive! He healed Thomas' heart and opened to him a new future. And in the years that followed, Thomas carried the Good News fearlessly all the way to India.

We've learned from experience that it's hard to quiet our hearts and pray when bad times come: we go numb as fear and despair grip our souls. The Lord is still there, but it doesn't *feel* like it. We'd like to run away, but there's nowhere to go that makes any sense. There's nothing we can do but speak our hurt and fear to the Lord and then be still and wait for his Wisdom to unfold ever so slowly.

If we trust, even though we cannot see, our waiting will be more than just marking time. The Spirit will walk with us through our agonies, guiding us through a kind of sorting: leaving at the roadside what's no longer needed, opening locked doors, uncovering what we will need for our journey. It's an anxious process, with many moments of jarring self-recognition and tearful letting go. But it opens the way to a future that's bigger than our past.

✝

The psalmist said so long ago: "Be stouthearted and wait for the Lord." Accept the silence and the darkness, the hurt and the feelings of powerlessness, and wait for the Lord. He is closer to you than you are to yourself, and he won't let you fall through the fingers of his great hand.

FRIENDSHIP IS YOUR LIFE'S WORK

A man was putting his groceries on the check-out counter, while a nearby drunk watched. "You're single, aren't you," said the drunk.

The man was startled and stared at the bacon, eggs, milk and bread on the counter. How did that say "single"? He couldn't see it, so he gave up and asked, "How did you know I'm single?"

The drunk replied, "Because you're ugly!"

✝

Ugly or not, we were made for love. Our greatest joys and sorrows come from our loves; and even on our crankiest days we long to talk with a friend we can trust. But often there is no friend. Even among the married, millions are friendless at the deepest level of their being, until at last they disappear unnoticed into the dark. That's always been the course of too many lives.

But Jesus came to change that. He helped us to see that our longing for friendship and love is no mere whim. It's woven into the fabric of our being; and God, who wove that fabric, *is* love. Since real love is expansive and cannot be corralled, it's impossible for God *not* to create us and love us! And since he lives at the center of our being, it's impossible for him ever to forget us.

We were made for God, who is *with* us, and *in* us, and *for* us. Communion with him and his people is the purpose of our life, and nothing less will ever fill our empty hearts.

This is what Jesus helped his friends to see on the road to Emmaus. They thought he was dead and that God had abandoned them. They thought they'd lost the one thing that matters: their loves. So Jesus listened to their hurt, fed their souls with his healing presence, and gave them back their loves - and thus their lives.

✝

Listen to the Spirit. You'll always know you're loved, and you'll never forget your life's work: building communion with God and his people. Let that holy work fill your days. It will be your joy and will bring you safely home.

HOW DOES GOD ACTUALLY
DEAL WITH US?

A crooked lawyer arrived at the gates of heaven, where St Peter asked: "Why should we let you in?" The lawyer was stumped but finally recalled that he'd once given a quarter to a beggar.

"That's true," said the angel Gabriel, "but hardly enough!"

"Wait, wait, there's more," cried the lawyer. "I tripped over a crippled child last week and gave him a quarter too."

Peter shook his head and asked Gabriel, "What should we do with him?"

"I say we give him back his 50 cents, and tell him to go to hell."

✝

Gabriel said it and we thought it! We're lucky that God doesn't think like us. *He* views us with the eyes of a father, a brother, and a mentor - Father, Son and Spirit. If we really get that, it will change the way *we* view one another. But too often it doesn't.

In Jesus' day, people viewed poverty, disease, and natural disasters, which we still call "acts of God," as God's punishment for sin. Hence they scorned the victims as morally corrupt and interpreted their own good luck as proof of their virtue: I'm rich, so I must be good!

They were wrong and Jesus repeatedly said so. But few listened, and so it continues: the poor get labeled as lazy, the homeless as drunks, and the victims of AIDS as the proper targets of divine wrath. That self-righteousness has no place in our hearts, so we need to look more closely at *how God actually works with us.*

Bad things happen to us all. Sometimes it's just bad luck (our house burns down), and sometimes it's the natural consequence of our bad choices (driving drunk earns a DUI), but *never* are our misfortunes the punitive acts of a vengeful God.

On the contrary, the Mentor-Spirit who dwells within us, continues the *healing* work of Jesus, softening our hearts, guiding our minds, and helping us to see the truth and to be true. We may ignore the Spirit and set a destructive course for ourselves, but the Spirit never abandons us. It stays near, suffers with us as we stumble, and then helps us find the heart to start anew. There is no vengeance in the Spirit, only the tender desire to help us find our way and grow whole.

✝

Listen to the Spirit and learn to shepherd the least of your brothers and sisters as the Spirit shepherds you. Together you will grow whole and find your way home.

THE PAINFUL SILENCES HAVE SOMETHING TO TELL YOU

A man was on his deathbed, drifting in and out of consciousness, when he was jarred awake by the aroma of his favorite chocolate chip cookies. "Just one more before I die," he said to himself. So he crawled downstairs and found hundreds of *those* cookies cooling on the table. He took one and it was heavenly. But as he reached for another, out of nowhere, a spatula smacked his hand, and he heard his wife's voice: "Hands off, Edgar! Those cookies are for the funeral!"

✝

At times the prospect of a funeral is almost a relief. Troubles close in upon us. The people and things we've counted on lose their magic. And the Lord is silent. Has he abandoned us? No, he never leaves. Is he punishing us for sins we've long forgotten? No, there's no vengeance in him.

Our feeling of abandonment is of our own making. For even the best of us let trivia distract us. We pin our hopes on silly things that cannot save us. Our connection to the Lord grows progressively weaker and perhaps even breaks. And then comes the silence, which exposes our need for the One we've forgotten, the only One who can fill our empty souls. That precious connection can be restored, but not with a simple change of mind. It will take time and our full attention, as the healing of any love always does.

But a broken connection is not the only source of God's silence. Sometimes as we look around us, we pray with great intensity and perhaps even indignation: "Lord, how can you let this be? Why don't you do something?" But the Lord doesn't respond, the silence is deafening, and for many that will be the end of the story: no more praying "because God doesn't listen."

But if we remain still and take the time to probe more deeply, the Lord's answer, which was there all along, will slowly rise into our consciousness: "I've already given you everything that's needed for *you* to do what you're asking *me* to do. I'll be with you at every step of the way, but you have to pick up your tools and use them."

✝

Even with his silences, the Lord draws us forward as a good parent does. Trust him. Give thanks for the power for good that he's placed in your hands. And take care to keep that precious bond strong: it's your lifeline and your first taste of heaven.

LEARN TO SEE YOURSELF THROUGH THE EYES OF GOD

A well-dressed man was walking down the street when a bum asked him for a handout. "Is it for liquor?" asked the man.

"No, sir. I don't drink."

"What about gambling?"

"I don't gamble."

"Well, surely it's not for golf."

"No," said the bum, "I don't play golf."

"Well then, why don't you come home with me for dinner."

"I'd really like to," said the bum, "but won't your wife be angry when she sees a bum at her table?"

"Of course she will," said the man, "but I want her to *see* what happens to a man when he *doesn't* gamble, drink and play golf."

✝

We can't help wonder what else went unexamined in that marriage. It's hard to *see* the truth, and even harder to *do* something about it. Many just give up, like Pilate, who sneered: "What *is* truth?" He'd given up caring, and that made it easy to send Jesus to the cross without a backward glance.

That kind of inner decay could happen to us, but it doesn't have to, because Jesus didn't leave us defenseless. The Spirit, who lives within us and knows us inside out, continues Jesus' healing work. The Spirit helps us see the clash of light and darkness within us and guides us towards wholeness, where all the parts of us will fit together and make sense.

But we resist the Spirit! We don't want to look at our *dark* side. It hurts. It's embarrassing. It says: get to work, change me! But we're not sure we *can* change. It's not a pretty picture, but not a surprise.

What *is* surprising is our resistance to seeing our *light* side - our very real progress despite so many obstacles. It *should* give us hope and spur us forward. But fear says, if you relax even for a moment, you'll backslide and be lost. So we ignore our hard-won successes, slowly lose heart, and get exactly what we feared: sadness and decline.

✝

The Spirit sees you as you really are: not done yet, but worth loving. Let your heart see what the Spirit sees; and step by step grow into the dream that God our Father dreamed for you so long ago.

ARE YOU GOOD NEWS OR BAD NEWS?

A man fell into a pit and couldn't get out, and everyone had something to say about it:

— Buddha said, "Pit is only a state of mind."

— The building inspector asked, "Do you have a permit for this pit?"

— Confucius say, "If listen to me, not fall into pit."

But Jesus said nothing at all. He just took the man by the hand and lifted him up.

†

That's what Jesus did all his life. He didn't just *tell* the Good News, he *was* good news for countless people, as he took their hands and didn't let go. And their hearts whispered: "God loves me and he doesn't intend to lose me." That experience is within our reach, because the Spirit of Jesus is with us always.

When Jesus ascended to a new life with the Father, his last words were to us all: "Share the Good News as I've shared it with you. Don't just talk it, 'walk' it, become it! Let your goodness bring hope and healing to everyone you touch." That's a daunting task for people who live on a treadmill and can't remember where they put their car keys.

Statistics tell us that the majority of violent crimes are committed against relatives and friends. And the same is true of our lesser cruelties: our prime victims are those nearest and dearest to us. So if we want to *be* good news, like Jesus, that's where we have to start, in our own backyard.

Every day we have to ask hard questions of ourselves: "Is her day a little less sad because I'm here, or have I added to her pain? Did I bring him healing or did I reopen old wounds? Was I good news today or bad news?" Sometimes the answer will make us smile and whisper, "Bless you, Lord, we did it together!" But other times, the answer will hurt: "I was bad news. Help me, Lord."

†

Real change is like turning an ocean liner. It takes time. So give it whatever time it needs, and don't try to travel alone. Take the Lord's hand, extend your hand to your neighbors, and make your way home together.

YOU NEED THE SPIRIT, SO MAKE THE TIME!

Helen Keller was born deaf, blind and mute - trapped in her own body. She seemed a girl without a future, when Anne Sullivan stepped into her life. But slowly they found a way to communicate. As time passed, Anne worried that she hadn't taught Helen about God. But how could she talk about God to someone who'd never seen God's world? So with great trepidation, she took Helen's hand and slowly signed to her about God who lived in her heart and loved her very much.

Helen paid close attention and then began to smile: "I've always known him," she said. "I just didn't know his name!"

†

So who's the blind one, Helen or most of us?

The Holy Spirit has lived within us from the moment of our birth, but like the apostles at the first Pentecost, most of us haven't noticed. Inner "noise" deafens us to the whispers of the Spirit. Restless desires absorb our energies. The Spirit is still here, but we haven't learned to listen.

The gospels describe the Spirit as "wind," invisible but powerful, ranging across the earth, breathing life, and whispering things we've never dreamed of. They say the Spirit is also "fire," hot and bright, able to set us ablaze with passion for life, burning away what's dead in us, giving us light when we're in darkness.

We need the Spirit. We need the silent conversation that can focus and energize our souls. *With* the Spirit, we can be fearless seekers of truth and builders of loves that last. But *without* the Spirit, our hearts will shrivel, and lives that could have been rich will never be.

So how do we find this Spirit who carries on the work of Jesus? We begin by shedding the images of God left over from childhood. God is not a sweet old grandpa in the sky or a policeman who's just waiting to catch us, or someone who can be bribed with prayers and promises. God is *mystery,* vast beyond all knowing, yet alive within us and drawing us near.

So we draw near. We silence the outer noises and calm the inner chatter, and with grateful hearts remember we're in the holy presence of God! He doesn't speak in words or riddles like the oracles of old. He doesn't give instant answers. But if we have the patience and the trust to rest with him awhile, he'll gently probe and stimulate our spirits and nudge us towards what is good and true.

✝

You *need* the Spirit, but like everybody else, you rarely *feel* you have the time. Make the time. Cap the noise. And with a trusting heart, *rest with him awhile*. It will change your day and your life.

REST YOUR WHOLE WEIGHT
ON THE LORD

Long ago, when the first missionary came to New Guinea, cannibalism was common. No one was safe. They didn't even have a word for "trust." So when Trinity Sunday came, the priest was stumped. The key line of the gospel was: "Whoever puts his trust in the Lord will not die." How do you explain that to people who don't trust anyone? But the priest had an idea. He leaned back in his chair with the front legs entirely off the ground and said to his assistant, "Tell me what I'm doing."

"You're resting your *whole* weight on the back legs," said the youth.

"That's it!" said the missionary, "Whoever rests his *whole* weight on the Lord will not die, but will have eternal life."

†

God didn't send Jesus to condemn us, but to wake us up and bring us to life. So why are we still so lifeless? What should we do? The missionary told us: rest your *whole* weight on the Lord.

That *doesn't* mean that if we trust the Lord, our cancer will disappear, our cranky neighbor will learn to smile, and our teens will jump out of bed because it's time for mass. No, that's *our* work. It's up to *us* to find a cure for cancer, convert our neighbor, and guide our teens to maturity. And God has already given us the tools.

But one thing is still missing, wisdom and courage. These are gifts of the Holy Spirit which come only to those who trust the Spirit. And that's a problem, because trust doesn't just happen. It's constructed over time in many conversations with the Spirit of Jesus within us. Those conversations slowly build a bond that finally enables us to speak from deep within: *"Lord, I know you love me and don't intend to lose me. I'll follow you anywhere."* That's what *receiving* the Spirit is like: arriving at a moment when we can rest our whole weight on the Lord and can see all things through ~~his eyes~~. the eyes of the Holy Spirit

✝

So where are *you* on this long journey to the Spirit? Is the driving force in your heart trust, or is it worry? Are you seriously engaged in conversation with the Spirit ~~of Jesus~~? Or are you trying to build a life all on your own? (Don't even think of it!)

Open your heart to the Spirit ~~of Jesus~~ within, and let the conversation begin in earnest. As it continues through good days and bad, through doubts and fears, more and more of your weight will come to rest on ~~Him~~, their eternal goodness, ~~his~~ peace will take hold of your soul, and you'll find that you have everything you need to finish well.

TO LOVE JESUS, YOU HAVE TO LOVE HIS FAMILY

A little boy looked up at the moon and asked, "Mom, is God in the moon?"

"Yes, Billy," she replied. "God is everywhere."

"Is he in that flower over there?"

"Yes, he is, son."

"Well, is God in my tummy?"

"Yes," said mom, wondering where this was leading.

"Mom," said the boy, "God wants an ice cream cone!"

✝

Little children aren't the only ones who get hungry. We're all hungry in many ways. Ice cream cones can fill some of our empty places, but our really big hungers demand more. We hunger for love that lasts, for friendships that won't go away, and for someone special to comfort us when we're sad and to hold our hand when we die.

We all hunger for love - for communion. And Jesus came to show us the *only way* to find it. It was profoundly simple: he *gave* himself to everyone he met. He gave his listening and his speaking, his embracing and his encouraging, his forgiving and his feeding. He gave his life day by day, year after year, and in the end he gave his dying. And to those who took his words to heart and walked his giving ways, he was able to bring healing, comfort, and strength, for those are the fruits of communion, the love that lasts.

Jesus' whole life was an offer of loving communion, and his giving himself in the Eucharist - Holy Communion - is part of that offer. But don't forget: Jesus doesn't travel alone. He brings all of God's people with him. If we want to receive him into our hearts, we have to receive them and share ourselves with them as well. (As in a marriage, if you truly love your spouse, you find a way to love your in-laws. You find a way!)

If we have *no room* in our hearts for God's people, our *Holy* Communion will be *no communion* at all and will bring us no lasting comfort or joy. But if we make room for them, our Holy Communion *will* be holy and healing, and the solitary sadness that afflicts so many of us will depart and never return.

There is no *real* life without love, and no *real* love without giving life away. There is no loving the *Lord* without loving his *people,* and no loving his people without giving part of your life to them. Remember that, and your life will always be full.

Ordinary 14 - A
Matthew 11:25-30

INSTEAD OF RUNNING, LET HIM GUIDE YOU *THROUGH* YOUR TROUBLES

A man was at the end of his rope and, as a last resort, decided to try a method of prayer known as "lucky dipping." He closed his eyes, opened his bible at random, and then let his fingers find their way. Whatever verse they came to rest on would be God's answer. When he opened his eyes, he was shocked to read: "Judas went out and hanged himself." Surely that couldn't be God's answer, so he shut his eyes and dipped again. This time it read: "Go thou and do likewise."

†

We all have our troubles, some we've made for ourselves while others just showed up. They wear us down and leave us feeling trapped. Jesus knew that, and he showed us a different path: "Come to me," he said, "all you who labor and are burdened, and I will give you rest." He wasn't promising to take away our troubles. He was offering us a partnership for dealing with them: "Take my yoke upon you and learn from me," he said, "and your soul will find rest."

In Jesus' day, everyone knew that a farmer put a yoke on an ox so he could guide it. Otherwise the plowing would be chaotic, and the day would be wasted. So Jesus was giving us an alternative to running away from our troubles or just wandering about aimlessly. "If you are connected to me," he said, "I can help you see what God sees: an honest path *through* your hurts and troubles. And I can give you the energy to keep going and not give up halfway."

You'll get battered along the road, but you'll get where you need to go. And you'll discover that in the process you've grown stronger, wiser, and kinder than you were before your troubles came. Even if the hurts and struggles continue for the rest of your life, you'll find peace, and the Lord, who is always near, will refresh you.

That is Jesus' promise: "Come to me, take my yoke upon you, and you'll find rest and peace."

✝

Listen to him. He knows the way, and he'll help you to find it.

SET DOWN DEEP ROOTS IN GOOD SOIL

At a dance, a young man struck up a conversation with an attractive young woman. After three dances, he strutted over to his buddy with a scrap of paper in his hand: "She works at the phone company, and I think she likes me, because she gave me her private number."

"Wow!" said his buddy, green with envy. "Let's see." So he unfolded the paper and read it aloud: "Dial Operator."

✝

Sometimes there's a lot less there than meets the eye!

At times we could say that about our lives: what have we got to show for all our years of living? Why isn't there *more* to us? Those are painful questions, but their urgency can open our souls to what Jesus has been telling us for so long: "If you want a rich, full life, 'the 30, 60, 100-fold' of the gospels, you have to put down roots - deep roots - in good soil."

That makes such sense, but it runs contrary to so much of who we are. We have a short attention span and a low threshold of boredom. The half-life of our enthusiasms is measured in weeks not years. (Check your garage and your closet for the evidence!) Like birds of prey, we scan the horizon for new looks and better offers. Day after day, we keep moving, hoping for something better, but changing nothing.

But even when we're *ready* to commit ourselves, there's still one more question. *Where* do we plant our hearts? What's worth a life? For most people, the main commitment is to a lifestyle, pursued with "gusto" of course. That's awfully shallow soil to plant a whole life in, and what grows there is bound to disappoint.

So where *do* we put down our roots? In the Lord, the only One who's big enough to satisfy all our longings. But *how* do we root ourselves in the One we can't even see? By planting our roots in the midst of his people whom we *can* see, for he is alive and waiting for us in every one of them.

✝

Commit your heart to nurturing God's people and building good bridges to bind them together. You'll find God, and with him the rich, full life that you've always hoped for.

GIVE THE GIFT OF GROWING TIME

At times, just living with one another can bring us to new highs of exasperation, and we can find ourselves saying:

— that person is depriving some village of an idiot, or

— if he were any more passive, we'd have to water him twice a week, or

— it takes him an hour and a half to watch "60 Minutes," or

— people like that should not be allowed to breed!

✝

Hard words, but haven't we *all* earned them at times? Why is that, even for the best of us? That's what those farmers were asking in Jesus' parable about the field they'd sowed with good seed but which came up half weeds: "Where did all those weeds come from?

It's a mystery we face every day, as we look at ourselves and one another: how can such good people strive so hard and yet screw up so badly? It's the human condition: God gave us life and the ability to grow, but we're not done yet. And what's more, we're not supposed to be!

There *is* no perfect spouse, child, friend, or golf pro. And there never will be in this life. So what do we do with the gravelly parts of our relationships and with our frustrations at our own failures?

We watch Jesus! He had a clear fix on everyone around him. He knew Peter was impulsive and a blowhard, but he saw something more in him. He knew Judas was superficial and a thief, but he saw something more in him too. In every case, Jesus focused on that "something more" and hoped in it mightily. Peter took that gift to heart and began to change. Judas did not.

As we struggle with one another's weaknesses, the Lord doesn't expect instant perfection. What he does expect is humble compassion, which looks at our neighbor and says *in truth*, "I've probably done worse, so I'm in no position to throw stones. But I can give the gift of hope - and growing time. That 'weed' may yet turn into a 'rose'."

As we hope in one another and take the time to walk side by side, our hope will usually bear fruit, not all at once, but truly - if we persevere. And our neighbors won't be the only ones who change. Our hoping for them and our walking with them will change our own hearts. Giving ourselves away always makes us more, not less. The gift we give always comes back to us.

✝

Give the gift of hope - and of growing time - to your neighbor and to yourself. Receive each day gratefully, and leave the sorting out to God.

LEARN TO LISTEN WITH YOUR HEART

An elderly woman was upset because her husband was ignoring her. So she called her pastor, who came for a visit. "He never hugs or kisses me or tells me he loves me," she said tearfully as her husband slugged down another beer and turned up the TV.

To get his attention, the priest put his arms around the old woman, gave her a warm hug and a kiss, and then turned to the husband: "See what I did? Your wife needs something like that at least twice a week."

"Fine," said the old boy, "I'll bring her to see you on Tuesdays and Thursdays."

✝

Not listening is a habit as old as Adam and Eve. That's why King Solomon's prayer on the eve of his coronation is so startling. God offered him unlimited power and riches, but all Solomon asked for was an understanding heart, a heart that could listen.

He wanted to be like God: reaching beyond himself, hearing the inside of life where the Spirit dwells, and feeling the sorrows and longings deep in people's souls. He wanted to find the wisdom to be a healer and a protector of the weak.

It was a noble prayer, and God answered it: the wisdom of Solomon became legendary, even to our own day. But there was tragedy waiting for him, as it had for his father, King David: the wisdom wouldn't last. As the years passed, his youthful idealism slowly gave way to self-indulgence and cynicism. And when at last he came to die, the only voice he was listening to was his own. And there was little truth in it.

We've walked many miles since our first youthful attempts to imagine our future selves and to see what's worth valuing and what's not. For most of us, a listening heart was not on our short list. So we have to *learn the habit* of listening to the Spirit of Jesus, who is always near and always listening to us. That gentle Spirit can calm our hearts to listen to our own souls and to one another, and to lay claim to a deeper wisdom that will translate into love and joy.

†

Learn to listen with your heart. Wisdom, kindness, and peace will surely follow.

YOU ALREADY HAVE WHAT YOU NEED

A student once asked the famous anthropologist Margaret Mead what was the earliest evidence of civilization. He expected her to say something like a clay pot, a fish hook, or a grinding stone. But instead she pointed to a healed femur and explained that a person with a broken femur couldn't hunt or gather or even run away from danger. On his own, he'd last only a few days. So a *healed* femur meant that someone else did the hunting and gathering and defending until the victim's leg could heal. The first sign of real civilization: someone looking beyond his own needs to care for another.

†

So how civilized are *we*? So much of life seems beyond our control, not just the climate or the economy or the antics of our leaders, but even the dynamics of our own families. We can feel powerless to make things better.

Jesus had those feelings at times. He was giving his all, but many weren't listening. And then he got word of John the Baptist's terrible death. He was devastated and *needed* to be alone with his Father. But the crowd soon found him.

What would he do? Give up and go home? It happens every day. But what *could* he do? He could give them a new life, *if* he could bring himself to reach beyond his hurt and his weariness. And that's what he did by the power of the Spirit alive within him. He took those people to his heart and fed their wounded spirits. He set them on a new course and gave them hope.

There will never be a *convenient* time for us to reach beyond ourselves. We'll always be tired or in the middle of something. "Life is what happens while we're making plans." So what will we do when a "broken femur" shows up? We'll be tempted to say that it's more than we can handle. But then we'll hear the voice of the Spirit who spoke to Jesus so long ago: "You already have what you need to do this. If you ask, I will help you reach beyond yourself and *use* your gifts for my people."

✝

Name your gifts, and claim them with a heart that's glad to have something valuable to share. Then ask the Spirit to help you reach beyond yourself. That prayer is always answered and never turned away!

Ordinary 19 - A
Matthew 14:22-33

YOU CAN DO THE IMPOSSIBLE AND ENDURE THE UNENDURABLE

A Wall Street banker bought a huge cattle ranch out West. Some friends came to visit and asked if the place had a name. "Well," he said, "I wanted to name it the BAR-J. My wife favored SUZY-Q. One son liked the FLYING-W, and the other wanted the LAZY-Y. So we're calling it the BAR-J SUZY-Q FLYING-W LAZY-Y."

"But where are all your cattle?" the friends asked.

"Well," he said sheepishly, "none of them survived the branding."

✝

Life is a gift, but it's no picnic, even for the best and the brightest. Every day many folks sink beneath the waves and drown in their troubles. How many times we've seen a young couple exchange their vows all bright eyed and hopeful, and then, as the years passed, watched their light grow dim and their dreams go sour. How many times we've held a child in our arms and imagined all the possibilities within the reach of its tiny hands, and then watched the possibilities elude the grasp of those now grown-up hands, and seen them grow tired and cease to reach out at all. Too many times.

Why is it that so many people drown in their troubles? The gospel gives us a clue. Jesus invited Peter to do something entirely beyond his own powers. "Come," he said, "walk on the water!" And that's exactly what Peter did. He stepped out of the boat - can you imagine that first step! - and began to walk across those roiling waters to Jesus.

He was already halfway there when suddenly he was overwhelmed by the crash of the waves and the roar of the wind and said to himself, "This is crazy. I can't walk on water." And he sank like a rock. But he had indeed walked on water. He'd done the impossible, because his eyes and his heart had been fixed on Jesus. He sank only when he lost his focus on the Lord.

The Lord is inviting us to do great deeds, to build good lives and powerful loves, not off in some safe haven, but here amidst all the winds and waves that life can serve up. And he's promising more than mere survival. He's promising us his own peace, even while life is battering us. How can that be? How do we find the power to endure the unendurable and to do the impossible? We find it as Peter did, by keeping our eyes and hearts fixed on Jesus.

Jesus endured the unendurable. Then he died. But he wasn't destroyed. He rose from the dead.

✝

Fix your eyes and your heart on him; never look away! In your life's journey, you'll endure many deaths, many crushing hurts. We all do. But if your eyes and your heart are his, you will rise with him, again and again, until at last you walk with him into eternity.

Ordinary 20 – A
Matthew 18:15-17

NAME IT, CLAIM IT, FEEL IT, FIX IT

Two boys were playing football when one of them was attacked by a rabid dog. Thinking fast, his pal ripped a board from a picket fence, wedged it inside the dog's collar and twisted it, breaking its neck! A reporter saw it all and wrote a dramatic headline: *Brave Padres Fan Saves Friend From Vicious Beast!*

"But I'm not a Padres fan," objected the boy. The man rewrote his headline: *Little Chargers Fan Rescues Friend From Rabid Dog!*

"I'm not a Chargers fan either."

"So what *is* your team?" asked the reporter.

"The Raiders!" And that brought forth a very different headline: *Ruthless Child Destroys Beloved Family Pet!*

✝

From "friend" to "enemy" in 60 seconds! It happens every day. A mistake is made, we close our hearts, and God's big family shrinks a little smaller.

We often *do* thoughtless and hurtful things, and just as often we *fail to do* the good we owe. Sometimes it's just a small thing: sending a wrong order, not returning a call. But sometimes it's a tragedy: removing the wrong lung, keeping silent while the innocent are punished. The only sin-free zone in the whole world is the inside of a sealed coffin! So we have to become experts at reconciliation, whether we're the villain or the victim. (By the way, we're always the first victim of our own misdeeds, shrinking our own hearts as we are heartless towards others.)

Jesus pointed the way, as he reached out to people weighed down by sins they often couldn't see. He was always compassionate, but *he didn't do cover-ups!* Instead he helped people to own the truth: to name it, claim it, feel it, and then fix it.

He helped us to understand that being a little sorry isn't enough. The villain has to surrender his defiant denial ("it was her fault" or "he asked for it"); and the victim has to surrender her self-righteous victimhood ("How could he *do* such a thing?"). The whole truth must be spoken - in love - until the sinner can *feel* his victim's hurt, and the victim can *see* that he's felt it and won't do it again.

✝

True reconciliation always takes two: the villain and the victim, both owning the truth, giving and receiving healing. This can take time; so make the time. Keep your eyes on Jesus, and *become a builder of honest peace!*

DO YOU KNOW *ABOUT* JESUS OR DO YOU KNOW *HIM?*

Bumblebees are intriguing to watch as they buzz around our gardens, but they're surely not at the top of nature's IQ list. If you drop one of them into an empty water glass, it will never escape, because it never looks up to see the sky. Instead, it searches frantically for a non-existent escape hatch at the bottom of the glass. And eventually its buzzing ceases.

✝

We're a lot smarter than bumblebees, but sometimes we're remarkably obtuse. That's why Jesus pressed his disciples with a pointed question: "Who do you think I am?" They weren't theologians, so they had to respond from their hearts. And so do we, for that's where the real answer lies.

Knowing Jesus is very different from just knowing *about* him - any atheist can read the gospels. *Knowing* Jesus takes nothing less than a bonding of hearts that changes our inner landscape: his thoughts become our thoughts; his loves become our loves.

That's how it's supposed to be between Jesus and us. So after all our years as "Christians," it's fair for him to ask: "Do you *know* me?" If we *do,* and his imprint is on our hearts, the evidence will speak for itself. And it will sound something like this:

+ Every morning, when I open my eyes, I'm glad to be alive.

+ I'm not afraid, because I know the Lord loves me and doesn't intend to lose me.

+ He's blessed me with everything I need to make a good life.

+ The people around me are thriving, because I love them even on their bad days.

+ I know I'm not done yet, but I'm getting better, because He is my strength.

✝

If you *know* Jesus and carry him in your heart, that's who you are. And that's who you'll see every time you look in the mirror.

WHY DID JESUS HAVE TO DIE?

In their ongoing search for cheap programming, the TV networks are now inviting us to watch hoarders on their sorry road to self-destruction. Rich or poor, they're driven by fear of want, and they cling to whatever they get their hands on, regardless of need or usefulness: towers of old newspapers, mounds of unused clothing, a menagerie of cats, dogs, birds and gerbils. Room by room they lose their homes, but still they cling to the stuff that's stealing their life.

†

Jesus warned us about this long ago: "What would it profit a man to gain the whole world and lose his own life?" That warning should lead us to think more deeply about why we *needed* him to come and why he *had* to die.

St Paul explained Jesus' mission with a commercial metaphor: God sent Jesus to pay off the infinite debt incurred by our sins. He had to "ransom us" *from our Father.*

That doesn't sound very fatherly!

The Franciscan explanation makes better sense. It says that *God sent Jesus to make his love for us so tangible and so compelling, that it would draw us out of ourselves and our petty entanglements and into a larger life of love.*

That makes sense, but did Jesus *have* to die to achieve it?

His enemies were plotting to kill him, because he said Jewish law was inadequate as a path to God. He could have fled and allowed their loveless view of God to prevail. But that would betray his teaching that *love is the only road to God*. He couldn't do that to us. So as the Eucharistic prayer says, he freely accepted death on the cross.

By keeping faith with us despite the cost, Jesus called us out of ourselves and into a bigger life with God and his people. No ransom, no debt payment, just God's son showing us that loving without counting *is* the one thing that matters and the only thing that lasts.

✝

Keep your eyes on Jesus, and don't be afraid to go wherever love leads you. Learn to give yourself away, "for it is in giving that we receive, and in dying that we are born to eternal life."

REAL LOVE IS SELF-TRANSCENDING AND SELF-CORRECTING

An elderly spinster died and left instructions that there be no pallbearers at her funeral. Her reasons were deeply felt: "They *didn't* take me out when I was alive, and I won't *let* them take me out when I'm dead!"

†

Learning how to love and be loved is a lifelong project, but many of us never quite get started. Part of the problem is that we don't know what we're talking about. We use the word frivolously: "I love pizza! She loves caviar!" And we don't seem to know the difference between the real thing and the warm and fuzzy feelings that come and go with the speed of a hummingbird. (And when they *do* go, so do the marriages and other commitments based on such feelings.)

Real love doesn't just happen. It's a deliberate choice to promote the well-being of another. Whether it's a grocery clerk, our mother-in-law, or our child, and whether they're with us for only a minute, or a weekend, or a lifetime, the choice is always the same: to promote that person's well-being - or not.

Making the right choice *every time* isn't easy. We can get so caught up in our own thoughts and moods that they get splattered on whoever happens to be around. And too often our "radar" spots the hurtful word or deed just a millisecond *after* we've launched it. So we have to learn how to live consciously in the present, taking life one moment at a time, and pouring our best into each moment. That can happen, if we check our "compass" many times every day and humbly press our reset button as often as needed.

In one of his tragedies, Shakespeare laments the hero's having loved "not wisely, but too well." It's a very human problem: we can set out to promote another's well-being, and we can invest all we have, only to discover that our "love" was just about us. True love is self-transcending and self-correcting. It listens to the heart of the other and isn't distracted by its own inner chatter. It shares what it has, it doesn't keep records, and it never forgets, that even the smallest of things, wrapped in love, can give life.

✝

True love looks like Jesus, so keep your eyes on him. Remember how much *you* are loved, and then give yourself away - without counting.

HOW UNDERSTANDING IS YOUR HEART?

Three prisoners on death row had argued for years about who was the smartest. When at last their day of execution came, the first man was strapped into the chair, the switch was pulled, but nothing happened. So the warden commuted his sentence and set him free. The same thing happened to the second and he too was set free. Finally, the third was strapped in the chair, and again nothing happened. But before the warden could say a word, this "smart" guy interrupted: "Hey, dummies, can't you see? All you gotta do is cross the black wire with the yellow one..." And so they did!

✝

Even the smartest of us are astonishingly foolish at times. We do what we know isn't good for us. We repeat yesterday's mistakes with the accuracy of a xerox, and we make choices we know can't possibly lead to a happy day, much less a happy life. And yet, God dearly loves us, and so do many of his people.

It's not because they don't see our shortcomings. They see them all, but they see something more as well. Side by side with our flaws, they see the goodness we're trying to grow inside us. And, like God, our true friends say to themselves, she needs my understanding and my help. And that's what true friends give, understanding and help.

Jesus' parable about the man who was drowning in debt and had no way out is a shocking reminder of how desperate we all are for help and understanding. Yet, paradoxically, we're tempted every day to withhold from our neighbors the very help we know we need if we're to survive. We hold back our compassion, as if it were a non-renewable resource. And our lives are soured because of that.

There is no surer path to happiness and peace of heart than to spell out the full extent of our need for help and understanding, and then to use that as the measure for the help we're willing to extend to one another. In doing this we enlarge our own hearts and make them ready to receive all we need. Jesus said it perfectly. "The measure you measure with will be measured back to you." That's just the way that hearts work.

✝

May the measure you measure with be very large indeed.

EVEN IF THE NIGHT IS FALLING, IT'S NOT TOO LATE!

The Montana Department of Fish and Game is advising campers to be on the alert for bears while in the national forests. They're urging visitors to wear little bells to avoid startling bears. They also advise carrying pepper spray in case of close encounters. Department officials indicate that you can accurately determine the kind of bears in an area by observing their droppings. Black bear droppings are smaller and contain berries and occasionally squirrel fur. Grizzly bear droppings have bells in them and smell like pepper spray. So says the Department of Fish and Game!

†

On the face of it, Sunday's gospel seems to fit right in with the "wisdom" of the Department of Fish and Game: Pay the latecomers first to make sure that those who worked all day will know exactly how badly they got cheated! It seems unbelievably stupid, and it would be if the gospel were about labor relations. But it's not. It's about conversion.

Most of us were baptized as infants, and in the course of time we learned the rules (Thou shalt! Thou shalt not!), we learned the words (Our Father, Hail Mary), and we learned the moves (sit, stand, kneel). But lots of us never quite learned the Lord, never quite got him to the center of our lives.

Most of us have given the Lord a part of our lives, but we've also held back some parts, and even set some parts strictly off limits to him. The result is that we have unfinished business, and if we're at all alert to our inner life, that unfinished business makes us uneasy and less than happy with ourselves. What makes us even more uneasy is that in many cases we've been sitting on this unfinished business a long time.

That's what Sunday's gospel is about. It's about our having got to a point fairly "late in the day" with some of our life's work still unfinished or even unnamed. This strange gospel is Jesus' invitation not to despair at the lateness of the hour, but to come to work with him even now, though much of our day has already passed.

†

Jesus has been waiting for you so long. Open your heart, take his hand, and step forward into a new life now, even if the shadows of evening are far advanced.

WHAT DOES GOD EXPECT OF YOU?

An important monsignor arrived in heaven at the same time as a scruffy New York cab driver, and both were quickly assigned their new homes. The cabby got a mansion just blocks from the throne of God, while the monsignor got a third-floor walk-up on the outskirts. He was outraged: "I devoted my entire life to God, and this is what I get?"

But St Peter was firm: "We reward *results* here. Don't you recall what happened when you gave sermons?" The monsignor blushed and admitted that everyone fell asleep. "Exactly," said Peter. "On the other hand, when people rode in this man's cab, they prayed!"

✝

Results matter. So what are the results that God expects from us? A mistake-free life? An unblotted copybook? A resume chock full of nothing but good deeds - all cashews and no peanuts? God knows us better than that. As a good father, he understands that every one of us starts with a "blank blackboard" and has to learn even the simplest things from scratch. We're constantly faced with challenges we hadn't anticipated and often find ourselves baffled and befuddled.

So we proceed as best we can, by trial and error, sometimes foolishly over-committing, other times nervously under-committing, getting some things just right, and making other choices that will never work. We're like those sons in the gospel, wanting to make good lives, but getting our yeses and noes all tangled up.

That's the *reality* of our lives; so what *does* God expect? More than anything else, he wants us to get serious about learning how to listen to his Spirit deep inside us, as he gently nudges us towards what is good and true. If we learn to listen well, the power of his Goodness will help us to see our mistakes and to turn wrong into right. And where we've made good choices, he'll help us to grow into our commitments and to invest our whole selves in making them come true. Through it all, he'll bless us with the quiet kindness of his good people.

✝

So don't ever give in to fear or despair as you look at your life. Be of good cheer. You have what you need: many good gifts, many caring friends, and the Lord himself alive in your heart. He has the patience of a very dear father, so take his hand and step forward. You're on sold ground!

ARE YOU TOO OFTEN THE ONLY ONE WHO COUNTS?

Two old friends were hiking in the woods when one was bitten by a rattle-snake. Without a moment's delay, his buddy ran ten miles to find a doctor, but he was delivering a baby. "I can't leave," said the doc. "But all you have to do is take a knife, cut a little X where the bite is, and suck out the poison. Your friend will be fine."

The young man had turned white as a sheet, but he ran the ten miles back to his friend who asked urgently, "What did the doc say?"

His buddy replied tearfully: "He says you're going to die."

✝

He did it *his* way, like the tenants in Jesus' parable about tenants who'd grown accustomed to *taking* what they wanted and having their own way. When the owner asked for his rent, they felt put upon and killed his messengers! It was a vicious act, but there's something about it that should seem familiar: *taking* more than is ours and resenting any challenge.

We do many things well, and for the most part, we're assets to our community. But at times we step outside these laudable patterns and act as if *we* are the only ones who matter. For some of us, it happens when we get behind the wheel: watch out, world, the road is mine! For the bullies and control freaks among us, all we need is to spot someone weaker than ourselves. For others, it's money that causes us to speak the big lie: "It's mine, *all mine*, and I'll do with it as *I* please." The list is long, but the pattern is always the same: I'm the only one who counts and I *will* have my way, no matter the consequences for the rest of God's family.

And worse yet, because we do so many things well, we may not tag *these* sins for what they are. But St Paul did, as famously quoted in Handel's *Messiah*: "All we, like sheep, have gone astray, *every one to his own way*."

That should send us back to Jesus on the run, for he is the ultimate mirror for our souls. As we walk with him through the gospels, he leaves no doubt as to our real life's work: share one another's burdens, for you were not made to walk alone; protect the weak, for you too are weak; and give thanks always, for all you have is gift.

TAKE THE LORD AND HIS BIG FAMILY TO YOUR HEART

A courtly old gent walked into an upscale restaurant. He was impeccably dressed and spotted an equally handsome older woman at the bar. "May I join you?" he asked with a bow.

"By all means!" she smiled.

He ordered a drink, took a sip, and then looked at the lady intently: "So tell me," he said, "do I come here often?"

✝

It's easy to lose our way, and not just in old age. Terrible tragedies - sudden death, fire, bankruptcy - can upend our lives, and so can major transitions, like divorce or retirement. Suddenly our brain is awash with questions: Who am I? What's my life for? How can I go on? It's an agonizing experience, but it's also a chance to set down deep roots in the *right* place, perhaps for the first time.

God's big family is that right place. The first pages of almost every basic ethics text underscore what we know from experience: we're social beings. We're not made to live in isolation; we're made for love, connection, communion, and our lives won't work without it. But many of us try anyway, living on the far edges of community, disengaged from the needs and travails of others, resenting any claims on our time and resources, and ready to flee into the "safety" of solitude at a moment's notice. It's a recipe for a failed life.

Jesus showed us a better way: "Love God with all your heart; and love your neighbor as yourself." That kind of love doesn't think it's done when it has kind thoughts and good wishes for others. It steps forward and acts, because it knows that real love means sharing one another's burdens and giving ourselves into making lives better.

By virtue of birth, we're all members of God's family, but it's quite a different matter to be *participating* members. It's intrinsically messy and often exhausting, but it grounds our lives as nothing else can, for that's where we find God. And it's where we learn to be more than mere acquaintances, but friends who are faithful unto eternity.

†

Don't settle for a life that may appear to be full but is just plain empty. Take the Lord and his people to your heart, and keep them there. Your soul will never be hungry again.

YOU HAVE WHAT'S NEEDED. ARE YOU GIVING IT?

A man walked into a roof-top bar and heard someone talking about the unique wind currents there. "What's so special about them?" he asked.

"Let me show you," said the speaker who jumped out the window, did a couple of loops, and then returned to his drink. "Isn't that great! You can do the same thing."

After a few more drinks, the other man decided that perhaps he could. So he jumped out the window ...and dropped like a rock. The bartender shook his head in disgust: "Superman, you're really mean when you're drunk."

†

Most of us are neither mean nor drunks. But avoiding notable nastiness isn't enough to make a life. For that, we need to follow Jesus. "Give to Caesar what is Caesar's," he says, "but *give to God what is God's.*"

Everything we have is God's. So how do we give it back? By praying twenty hours a day? Or perhaps throwing ourselves on a live grenade to save a friend? Nothing so dramatic. What God wants is for us to give our *selves* to his people, helping those who need help and giving life to those who need life. It begins with paying closer attention to those around us and making a habit of asking: How's he doing? What does she need right now? How can I help?

We can't turn back the clock and prevent accidents, restore fortunes, or raise the dead. But most of what people really need is within our power to give:

— Some of our neighbors are crushed by burdens that would be bearable, if someone shared them. We can do that.

— Some have lost the Lord and need help to find their way home to him. We can give that.

— Some have caused terrible hurts and need to make amends, but don't know how. A kind word, gently spoken, can draw them out of the dark. We can do that.

— And sometimes, when the unthinkable happens and no words can help, a quiet, loving presence can bring healing. We can give that.

✝

Stay alert. Give people your undivided attention. You'll be surprised at what you see, and even more surprised at what you can give, if you embrace God's people, one person, one moment at a time.

REAL GOODNESS SPEAKS FOR ITSELF

A woman had six pre-school children who made every day an adventure. One morning her four-year-old started following her unrelentingly. When she stopped, he'd run into her; when she turned, she'd trip on him. "Wouldn't you like to go out and play?" she asked.

"No, I'd rather be here with you," he replied.

And so it continued until finally she asked, "Why are you doing this?"

"Well," he said, "our teacher told us to walk in Jesus' footsteps. But I can't see Jesus' footsteps, so I'm walking in yours."

✝

So where are *our* footsteps leading? Wherever it is, someone is almost certainly following us.

In a culture of cheap talk, with spin doctors always ready to explain away the inexplicable, lives that ring true command our attention and move us to say, "I wish *I* were like that." But that doesn't make it so. Every day many lose their way amidst the babble of vacant lives. And sometimes *we're* part of the problem, walking the wrong way on a one-way street and gathering up hapless followers along the way.

But it doesn't *have* to be that way. We *could* be part of the solution. The powerful example of our goodness could light the darkness that enshrouds so many aimless souls. We could give back what we have received.

Think of the good people who've left an enduring mark on our character and our way of life. Many, perhaps most of them, never offered a single word of advice. But their goodness was so real that it spoke for itself and drew us near, until we made it our own. To this day, parts of many who are long dead still live within us, not just in memory, but in the very fabric and fibre of our soul.

✝

The world longs for such gifts, so watch where your footsteps are leading. Someone is almost certainly following you.

Ordinary 31-A
Matthew 23:1-12

JESUS OR THE PHARISEES: WHICH ARE YOU?

Long ago, when nightfall enshrouded the world in darkness and a candle created only the narrowest of tunnels through the unknown, a blind man was taking his leave from friends and setting out for home. He asked for a candle. They thought it strange, for he *was* blind. But he explained: "If I were to fall and had no candle, I'd become a stumbling block. And that, I must never be."

✝

At some point quite early in life, each of us crosses an invisible line and chooses the kind of person *we'll* be. It's not the choice between architect or doctor, single or married, but the choice between giver or taker. As the years unfold, our silent choice becomes habit, rarely changed except by some powerful force outside ourselves, usually a great loss.

In the gospels, Jesus asks us to look more closely at the two sides of our choice. The Pharisee, the taker, is the dominant choice of our culture: praising the rules but not keeping them, seeing the weak but ignoring them, and grasping always for the best seats, the prime cuts, and the latest toys.

And then, there's the counter-cultural choice, Jesus the giver: walking gently upon the earth, striving to make life livable for all, and taking delight in sharing God's gifts, instead of hoarding them.

Which are we, givers or takers? Most of us are hyphenated: taker-givers or giver-takers. So how do we move from conflicted lives to the giving ways of Jesus? Obsessing with trivia, such as too many desserts or distractions in prayers, won't get us there. We have to look at the *larger habits* that are impoverishing us, even if we haven't noticed them. Here are four examples:

1) *Needing* to "win," to look better than all the rest, and to catch everyone else's mistakes. It changes all of life into a battlefield.

2) Thinking that our *wants* are needs. Wants are bottomless pits.

3) Letting our souls be eaten up by *fear, resentment, or regret.*

4) Thinking like the early Israelites, whose love and concern stopped at their property lines. *"Not my problem,"* is the byword.

Some part of *each* of these habits is alive in *all* of us, and we need to be done with them all. But they'll leave a vacuum behind. Only one thing can fill it: a realization that God loves us and wants us to be with him forever. Once we "get" that, not just in the head but in the heart, we're free, and our heart explodes in gratitude: we have everything that matters, and those old habits have no power anymore!

✝

Take life a moment at a time; love God *and his people* with all your heart; and give thanks always. The joy and the peace you've always desired will be yours!

WHAT WORD WILL YOUR HEART SPEAK WHEN YOU COME BEFORE GOD?

Whenever we hear of a friend or some public figure dying, our minds eventually turn to our own death: will I be very old or still young? Will it be sudden? Will I linger? So many questions come to mind, but we rarely ask the one that really matters: what kind of *person* will I be on the day I die?

There was a time when we imagined great ledgers being brought forth and divine auditors making a final tally of our deeds and misdeeds. But there will *be* no ledgers, and no auditors either, just the hearts that we've created across a lifetime. They're all that's needed, for every thought, word and deed of ours will have left its mark on them. *We'll have become what we had in our heart* when we thought and spoke and acted. And when we come before God, the heart that we've made will speak for itself. It cannot lie; it is what it is - for good or ill.

Finding our way home to God isn't about amassing credits in heaven's ledgers: so many churches visited, prayers said, and contributions made to the church. It's about loving so deeply that our hearts grow larger and more open and more receptive. So what does that love look like?

Love always wants what's best and is ready to do what's needed. It has staying power, and doesn't walk away when trouble comes. Love knows when to act, and when to do nothing at all. It knows that motive is everything:

a gift given in love will expand the heart, but the same gift made selfishly will shrink it. So learning to love means learning to probe our motives, asking often: Is this just about me? Why am I doing this? Why am I about to say that? Honest self-probing can prevent mortal damage, not only to others but to our own blind hearts.

Given the chance, real love finds its way into every corner of the heart and leaves its mark there. But we have to give it that chance!

✝

What is the defining word that your heart will speak, when at last it stands before God? Will it be "love" or just "me"? It all depends on what you've taught it across a lifetime.

DIG UP YOUR BURIED TREASURE AND SPEND IT ON YOUR NEIGHBORS!

There once was a mouse who was so afraid of a cat that a kindly magician changed him into a cat! But soon his fears focused on a dog. The magician turned him into a dog, but then he obsessed about a panther. "One more chance!" warned the magician, who turned him into a panther. But then the ex-mouse had nightmares about a hunter. In disgust, the magician turned him back to a mouse: "Nothing I do will ever make a difference," he said, "because you'll always have the heart of a mouse."

†

We've been entrusted with a unique treasure, the gift of life, which opens to us a world of possibilities. But like the lazy student who chooses a useless class for an easy "A", we often let what's easy or near at hand make our choices for us. And thus we never even see most of our gifts and never experience the joy of watching them grow and bring life to others.

Why *is* that? The legend of the mouse suggests an answer: the greatest of talents will do us no good if we have the heart of a mouse. It's too easy to be like the lazy servant in the gospel and let fear or simple lassitude control our destiny. And the result is a life that's smaller than it could have been, turned in upon itself, and happy to settle for just surviving.

But even if that *is* the story of too much of our past, there's no reason to say "too late" and declare our lives over. Every stage of life has its own opportunities for growing and expanding our hearts - even very late in life. Many doors have long since closed, but many are wide open and beckoning to us. Will we step forward now and find them? We will if we can say honestly:

— I greet every day with a glad and thankful heart.

— I live in the present and don't get distracted by mourning the past.

— I know that God has already put everything I need within my reach.

— I know that everything I have was made for sharing.

— Every day I watch for the Spirit's guidance to where I'm needed.

✝

Dig up your buried treasure and spend it on your neighbors. Help them to do the same. For both of you, the world will grow larger. And so will your joy.

MERCY GATHERS AND DOES NOT SCATTER

Many years ago, Dorothy Day was at one of her Catholic Worker Homes, listening intently to a homeless woman. A distinguished gentleman appeared and stood nearby, waiting for her to leave the woman and give *him* her full attention. But Dorothy didn't do that. She stayed with the one who needed her - for as long as she was needed. Only then did she look up and ask the gentleman in all sincerity, "Are you here to speak with one of us?" He was startled by her humility, but even more by her mercy: giving herself to the most desperate of God's children.

✝

St Thomas Aquinas said that mercy is the defining attribute of God. "Mercy" comes from the Hebrew word for womb! God is "motherly," and like a good mother makes no distinction between the "worthy" and the "unworthy." With kindly forbearance, God welcomes everyone into the shelter of his heart. He loves each of us - even those who killed his son - as if we were the only persons in the world.

This communion with God and his people is our life's goal, as the ancient hymn reminds us: "Just as many kernels of grain are gathered into one bread, so we are gathered into the body of Christ." But this coming together doesn't just happen. We are gathered by mercy, not just God's mercy, but one another's as well. Mercy is little less than a miracle in a world of litigious, self-absorbed individuals intent upon having their way. *Mercy is love with hands, and its hands are wide open.* It gathers, and connects, and weaves us into a community of the forgiven.

But *who* are the hungry and thirsty, the abused and the abandoned in *our* lives? They don't all wear rags and live on the street. Many are nearby, even in our own families. They need, as do we all, the gift of merciful forbearance - every day!

✝

Jesus had the heart to watch for that need wherever it was. And that's what he asks of you now: watch for those who need *your* mercy. Take them to your heart, not because they've *earned* your kindness, but simply because they're God's children - and *your* brothers and sisters.

CYCLE B

GET TO KNOW YOURSELF WHILE THERE'S STILL TIME

There once was a clever frog who hired a pair of geese to fly him to Florida for the winter. He tied each end of a long cord to one of the geese, took the center of the cord in his mouth, and signaled for takeoff. The flight went well until a boy spotted the frog sailing through the sky. "Wow!" he cried. "I wonder who thought of that!"

Froggie just couldn't resist answering: "I did!" And seconds later, he was just another grease spot on a parking lot in West Virginia.

✝

We've been living with ourselves for quite awhile now and have an abundance of personal data at our fingertips: our height, weight, date of birth, shoe size, food preferences, favorite colors, bank balance, and more. But with all that, we may still be as lacking in self knowledge as that braggart frog. That's why Jesus warned us so sternly: "Wake up!"

A good place to start is with some probing questions:

1. what do you value most?

2. what's your deepest fear?

3. what's your greatest gift?

4. what's your primary flaw?

5. how good a friend are you?

These are straightforward questions, but very few of us can give answers that capture the essence of us. It's not because we're trying to dissemble, but because we focus on peripheral things instead of the big defining patterns. Or we describe who we'd *like* to be rather than who we *are*. Or we say foolish things like, "I don't really have any gifts worth mentioning." No wonder Jesus is urging us to wake up!

Take the time to get to know yourself now. Go back to those five questions, and look for the big patterns - what you *usually* do, or don't do. That's where the truth lies, not in the exceptions. Focus on deeds, not wishes or plans. Seek out people who love you enough to tell you the truth. As you get to know yourself better, you can get better. But it's going to take time.

Recognize how you experience Gods presence
& how you act from that experience

Draw near to Jesus and, with open eyes and a trusting heart, take this journey with him one day at a time. You have nothing to fear: his love has no limits.

JESUS IS OUR BRIDGE TO THE FATHER

A group of 40ish girlfriends agreed to meet for lunch at Chez Henri, because the waiters were young and cute. They returned ten years later, at age 50, but this time it was the wine list that mattered.

At age 60, they decided to go back because it was quiet. Ten years later, their lunch priority was a handicapped ramp, and Chez Henri had the best one. And finally at age 80, they returned, "because we've never been there before"!

✝

Time flies and then, as scripture tells us, death breaks into our lives and robs us of everything we know: the home we've loved, the albums - none of it is ours anymore. All that remains is the invisible core of us, our heart, and within it the Spirit of Jesus, *our bridge to the Father.*

What then? Groping for an answer, St Paul said, "In our Father's house there are many mansions." And some imagined heaven as a gated community in the sky. He also said, "Eye has not seen nor ear heard what God has prepared for those who love him." And some imagined a celestial golf course where the sun always shines and no ball is ever lost.

Such speculations are useless, because heaven is *entirely beyond* our experience and our capacity even to imagine. God is mystery, and we have to let him translate our earthly experience into a form transferable to heaven. *This* St Paul understood: "I tell you a mystery," he said. "We shall all be changed, in a moment, in the twinkling of an eye."

This mysterious transformation is totally unearned and freely given.

But it can come only to hearts that are ready to *receive* it, hearts whose habitual love and compassion have "prepared the way for the Lord."

✝

What will be left of *you,* when everything you *have* finally disappears?

Only your *deepest self,* the heart you've made. Let the love and compassion that you've learned from Jesus define who you are. When your last day comes, you'll be ready, *"and the glory of the Lord will come in!"*

Advent 3 – B
Isaiah 61:1-2,10-11

JESUS CAME TO SET YOU FREE

A hyperactive little second grader brought home a disastrous report card. After stalling through dinner, he finally showed it to his parents. Dad shook his head and frowned: "Son, we're going to have to *do* something about these grades."

"But we *can't*, Dad," the boy said plaintively. "They're in ink!"

✝

He was trapped in a fixed idea and couldn't see a way out. It's happened to us all:

— Every family passes along an unsorted bag of ideas and values, many worth treasuring, others simply because they're there. (Does part of your inheritance need to go?)

— Most people decide who they are by age 25 and then spend the rest of their lives within the confines of that early vision. (Is yours large enough?)

— Diamonds may be forever, but some fears last even longer. (Have fears frozen you in place?)

— A heart without compassion leaves a trail of hurt and loneliness. (Are you your *own* first victim?)

In the course of a lifetime, we fall into many habits that prevent the emergence of communion and leave some of our best gifts unseen and untouched. But too often we don't notice. That takes probing and a strong heart, but as Isaiah reminds us, our Lord came to set captives free. And he would have come, even if *you* were the only one in trouble!

✝

Open your heart, and let his mercy draw you forward into the rich, full life for which you were made. Your soul will rejoice, and you'll wonder why you waited so long.

HE'S WHISPERING: COME TO ME!

Old Sam went to his doctor with a troubling question: "Can you detect mental decline in a man who still seems normal?"

"Oh, yes," said the doctor. "I ask a simple question, and if he fumbles, I know there's a problem. For example: Captain Cook made three trips around the globe and died during one of them. Which one?"

Sam thought for a minute and then laughed nervously: "Could you give me another example? I've never been that good at history."

✝

Keeping a solid grip on reality isn't easy - at any age. Fears and failures can deflate us to the point of despair, while an inflated ego can lure us into delusions of grandeur. We can see the latter in Israel's King David, the former shepherd boy, who forgot his humble origins and grandly announced to the Lord, "I'm going to build you a splendid house!"

The Lord just laughed: "The whole universe is mine," he said, "and you think I need *you* to build *me* a house?!" David's grandiosity was laughable, but his heart was in the right place. He wanted to do great things and to change the world for the better.

There's something of that in all of us, a longing to be good and to do great deeds, a longing for what's true and a desire to *be* true, a longing for the beautiful and a desire to make everything we touch beautiful. Even when our egos get carried away and we lose focus, the longing for what's good, true, and beautiful is always there. It's a whisper from God Himself: "Come to Me."

From the moment we drew our first breath, God has grasped our souls and drawn us towards His Goodness, towards the future He wants to share with us. As we stumble along, our hope falters at times and our egos run amuck, but even then our blundering ways are a response to his call: "Come to Me."

†

Give thanks for the ~~fatherly~~ love that never despairs of you and never loosens its grasp on your soul. Draw courage from his love, and know that he has a wonderful future waiting for you, where all your deepest longings will come true!

JESUS IS HOW MUCH GOD THINKS YOU'RE WORTH: EVERYTHING

There's an ancient Polynesian legend about a young man and woman who fell deeply in love. As was the custom, the groom had to buy his bride from her father, and the price was paid in cows. Depending upon the beauty of the bride, her father could demand as many as ten cows. For the rest of her life, each woman was known, for better or worse, as a three-cow, or a five- or six-cow bride.

Now as it happened, the bride in our story was no beauty. Indeed, the villagers agreed that a single cow - an old cow - would be a stretch. And so, with the whole village watching, the negotiation began. As expected, the bride's father asked for a single cow. But the groom refused! Instead, he insisted on giving a full ten cows! The villagers were shocked: "You traded away everything you owned for this miserable maiden. Why?!"

"Because," he replied, "I wanted her to know how much I think she's worth - everything."

It is said that, as the years passed, that "ten-cow bride" became the loveliest woman in the land.

†

As we recall the story of Jesus' birth and we remember where this wonderful child's life was headed, we have to ask God: "Why did you do it? Why did you give us all you have and hold nothing back? Why did you give us your own son?"

Out of the stillness, God whispers his response, "I gave you all I have, because I want you to know - and never forget - how much I think you are worth: Everything!"

PUT JESUS AT THE CENTER OF YOUR LIFE AND REST OF LIFE WILL MAKE SENSE

A young dad was trying to read a magazine, but his little girl kept interrupting. So he tore out a page with a map of the world on it, cut it into little pieces, and gave it to her: "Here's a puzzle, honey. Let's see if you can put it back together."

Within minutes, she had the map all put together. "How did you do it so fast?" asked her dad.

"Easy," she replied. "On the back of the map is a picture of Jesus. And when I got all of Jesus back where he belonged, the world was all put together."

✝

As we struggle to make sense of the world and to get our lives together, we often get discouraged by the evils that assault us from every side: heartless terrorists, greedy mortgage lenders, leaders who don't know how to lead. And we ask wearily, "Is this all there is?"

It's the same question the wise men asked 2000 years ago, but they didn't stop with just asking it. They traversed the world in search of someone who could give them an answer. And after a very long walk in the dark, they found Jesus.

He gave them new eyes with which to see the world and their own lives. Where all they'd seen before was a distant god who didn't much care about the chaos below, now they saw a loving God, who sent his Son to help us become family. With Jesus where he belonged, at the center of their hearts, the world came together for them: they knew where they were going and they knew how to get there.

✝

Put Jesus where he belongs: at the center of your life! Your days will make sense as they've never done before. Your first thought as you begin each day will be, "What would Jesus do?" And because you've got the question right, you're likely to get the answer right as well. You'll know what you need to do, and you'll have the courage to do it.

ARE YOU READY TO *MAKE* A BETTER FUTURE?

A wealthy matron was sailing on the newest ship of a luxury cruise line. Accustomed to being the center of attention, she was bombarding the captain with pointless questions. His responses were gracious, but his patience was finally exhausted when she said, "Tell me, Captain, how often do these ships sink?"

"Only once, madam," he replied. "Only once."

✝

As we look into our future, we have some questions of our own that need asking. They start with unfinished business, the heavy burden of the past that blocks our access to the happy future we're hoping for. Consider three examples:

— Mourning our losses is a healthy and necessary part of life. It's basic truth-telling: giving thanks for past gifts and accepting the reality that they won't be coming back. Healthy mourning has a beginning, a middle, and an end. But for some, mourning becomes a way of life, a surrender to the lie that there can be no joy after loss. Is mourning blocking your path to the future?

— Passion for justice is a virtue, and with it comes righteous anger when justice is violated. But anger all too easily morphes into bitterness that poisons the soul and strangles life. Is bitterness a roadblock to your future?

— Healthy fear is one of God's better gifts. It prevents us from driving with our eyes closed, it makes us study for exams, it teaches us the value of "no." But it can go insane and take control of whole areas of life, leaving us paralyzed and defeated. Is fear cutting you off from your future?

Fear, bitterness, and mourning are just a few of the malignant habits we may have accumulated across the years. They've been with us a long time, and they'll stay with us until we confront the real damage they do every day and then let the Spirit guide us toward a new freedom.

Confronting the baggage of our past is an indispensable prelude to the future we desire. But one thing more is needed, an act of insight and imagination that scans the landscape with new eyes: what gifts have I left lying fallow? Are there doors that I closed long ago and need to reopen for a closer look? If Solomon (cf Proverbs) was right in saying that "without a vision, people perish," am I in danger of perishing?

†

There's "gold" buried in those questions, but if the past is any guide, our temptation will be to ponder them awhile and then go for a nap. Don't do that! Make the crucial move from thinking to acting: form a plan with real strategies. The Spirit of Jesus will be with you at every turn, giving you courage, nudging you forward, and sharing your joy as you grow whole.

SEE WHAT GOD SEES IN YOU

A young woman and her sweet old grandma were sitting on the porch discussing a member of the family. "He's just no good," said the grand-daughter. "He's untrustworthy and lazy!"

"Yes, he has his problems," said grandma as she rocked back and forth, "but Jesus loves him."

"I'm not so sure of that," came the reply.

"Oh, yes," said the old lady. "Jesus loves him." She rocked some more and thought some more, and then added, "Of course, Jesus don't know him like *we* do..."

✝

What did Jesus see in Simon when they first met? He saw a man with a big heart and abundant enthusiasm, whose impulsiveness and bravado often got him in trouble. That was Simon! But Jesus saw something more: the seeds of greatness just waiting to come alive. So he looked Simon in the eye and said, "You are Peter, the rock. Come with me." Peter went with him, and in time he *became* a rock on whose goodness and strength countless others would rely.

The Lord is calling us, as he called Peter. It's not just a generic call, as in "y'all come." It's personal, for unlike everyone else in our life, the Lord grasps the very essence of us, the special qualities that make us like no other. He calls us by name: "Come with me. There's much you still need to learn before your journey is complete. But I will help you, if you come with me and let me show you the way."

†

Step outside yourself and see what the Lord sees in you - not just your mistakes and failures, but every one of your successes *and* the promise that they hold for the future. Let him help you find your next step, and go forward without looking back. You can't yet see where your journey will take you, but you can be sure of one thing: He will always be at your side. Don't be afraid. Be glad and step forward!

JESUS HAS A SECRET HE WANTS TO SHARE

A young man was walking on the beach when he stumbled on a magic lantern and liberated a grateful genie. "For your kindness," said the genie, "I'm going to send you three gifts this very afternoon: a miracle cure for all ailments, a huge diamond, and a dinner date with a famous movie star."

The boy was thrilled and rushed home, where his mother was waiting with bizarre news: "At noon someone delivered a barrel of chicken soup. Then a telegram said you've inherited a baseball field. And just now, MGM invited you to dinner with Lassie!"

✝

We've all been there: desperately longing for something life-changing, thinking for just for a moment that it's within our reach...and then back to desperate longing. That's why Jesus' invitation should command our attention. "Come with me," he says. "I have the secret of happiness that never ends: Love God with your whole heart, and love your neighbor as yourself."

Twelve simple words, full of hope, but fraught with danger if we tamper with their meaning. Yet every generation seems bent on tampering. Who can forget the folly of the seventies: "Love is never having to say you're sorry!" Wrong! Love is more than warm, fuzzy feelings and then doing as you please.

To love is to *act*, not just emote. It *wants* what's best for another, and it *acts* to make it happen. How many kind letters have we composed in our head but never mailed? How many noble deeds have we thought about but never done? Too many! They made us feel good, but they weren't love.

To love is to *choose,* but choosing wisely means looking beyond the surface for our neighbors' *real* needs and then sorting through our own complex motives. A good friend thinks hard before opting for tough love. A wise AIDS patient doesn't volunteer to give blood!

✝

Don't put your love on hold, waiting for the perfect time that may never come. Step outside yourself, and give yourself away early and often. It's a risky habit, but it's the only way you'll ever find the joy that Jesus promised, the joy you've always longed for.

DO YOU FEEL POWERLESS?

Garfield, that wily cat from the funny papers, was curled up in his cozy chair with a fire blazing and a beer in hand, while a fierce storm was raging outside. Through the window he saw one of his pals and gasped: "I can't just sit here and watch him freeze. I've got to *do* something!" With that he dashed to the window...and closed the blinds!

✝

This world of ours is a remarkable place, full of breathtaking beauty and goodness, from the tiniest of snowflakes to the tenderness of a mother's love. But there's another side to our world, a dark side of selfishness, hurt and hate, which sometimes leaves us on the doorstep of despair, numbed by feelings of powerlessness.

By his whole life and by his resurrection, Jesus gave us a very different vision of what our lives can be. On one occasion, he went to a synagogue and found there a man possessed by an "evil spirit." (That's a generic term for any evil that can take hold of a person from the inside.) The possessed man's screaming, cursing, and flailing about were shocking, and many left. But Jesus did not. He confronted the evil that had stolen that man's freedom. "Be quiet!" he said. "Have no more power over this man." And suddenly the man was set free and had a second chance at life.

At times we all *feel* powerless in the face of evil. But despite our feelings, God has *not* left us empty handed:

- He's given us the power to think, to strategize, to form a plan and to act.

- He's given us friends to walk with us and to keep us going.

- And he's given us the Spirit of Jesus, always there deep within, nudging us forward as we face what's broken or unfinished in us and in our world.

What more do we need?

✝

Don't let evil bully you into despair. Face it, wherever it is, starting with your own heart. Use the power that God has put in your hands, but use it with love. However long it may take, the Goodness that *is* God *will* prevail.

ARE YOU TRAPPED IN YOUR TROUBLES?

Three astronauts were going on a two-year space flight, and each was allotted 125 pounds of cargo. The first man's wife was just under 125 pounds, so he took her. The second had always wanted to learn Greek, so he took a box of Greek books and tapes. The third was a cigar fan, so he took 125 pounds of premium Havanas.

When they returned two years later, the first man stepped out with a big grin and a pair of twins. The second was beaming as he rattled off fluent Greek. But the third still had *all* his cigars and growled at the crowd: "Does *anybody* have a match?"

†

Trapped! We all know the feeling. Illness leaves us stranded in our own bodies. Grief takes hold of our hearts and won't let go. Guilt chokes the life out of us. A commitment that once seemed so right feels like a death sentence.

One day, as often happened, Jesus walked into a crowd of people who were trapped in their troubles, as *we* are so often. And he offered healing and freedom to every one of them. It was a joyful event. But for some, the joy didn't last, because they didn't take Jesus into their hearts where the real problems were. Sooner or later new troubles would strike and they'd be back to square one, this time without Jesus there to help.

But there were many others present that day for whom the encounter with Jesus was life-changing. They understood that he was offering more than just a feel-good escape from the troubles of the moment. He was offering *inner* healing and freedom that would last, because it had roots in the Lord whom they'd taken to their hearts.

Jesus offers *every one of us* that same healing and freedom:

- whenever we hear his Good News,

- whenever we share his Eucharist,

- whenever we calm our hearts to listen to his Spirit within us.

Our hurts and troubles may persist, but they'll lose their power to define and shape our lives. As we walk with Jesus day by day, we'll learn how to find purpose in our troubles instead of just railing against them. We won't be trapped in them anymore.

✝

Not a day goes by without the Lord holding out his hand and offering you healing and freedom. Take him to your heart once and for all. Even in the midst of troubles, you'll discover that you're free, and his joy will be yours!

FACING JESUS WILL LEAD US TO FACE OURSELVES

Bishop Fulton Sheen once visited a leper colony, where he planned to give a little silver cross to each of the 500 lepers. But when the first leper stepped forward, he had no *left* hand, and his *right* hand was covered with open sores. The bishop shuddered and drew back, holding the little cross at a safe distance *above* the leper's hand, and then just dropping it into his palm.

Later he said, "In a flash, I saw what I'd done. I realized there were 501 lepers there, and I was the worst! So I looked very hard at that little crucifix; and I knew what I had to do. I pressed my hand into the leper's hand with that tiny symbol of love between us. And then I did the same for all 500!"

✝

Deep within, all of us carry wounds from past mistakes. They haunt us, and we seem to be stuck with them. But Bishop Sheen's experience suggests a pathway to healing: facing Jesus will lead us to face ourselves and to find healing for what we've broken.

So close your eyes now, and call to mind a crucifix, perhaps one that's very special to you. Hold it in your mind's eye. Look at it very closely. If you take your time and don't hurry, Jesus will begin to speak to you from that cross. He'll explain that he *had* to die, not because God wanted revenge on a sinful world, but because freely giving his life was the only way to draw *you* near, the only way to prove that God's love for *you* has no limits and no preconditions. He just loves you! Even before you were born, he knew all the selfish things you'd do someday, yet he loved you anyway and *gave* his life so that you could *have* a life.

But as powerful as his love is, your healing can't begin until you *open* your heart to him. And that's what he's asking of you *now:* "Will you take me to your heart and make a permanent place there for me? Will you work with me to find healing for those old wounds of yours?"

✝

The choice is yours. Say, "Yes!" And keep your eyes on him always. As you work with him, you'll slowly grow into his likeness. Step by step, your heart *will* heal. And you too will become a healer!

WHAT YOU HAVE RECEIVED AS A GIFT, GIVE AS A GIFT

Three men were trying to cross a raging river, but failed repeatedly no matter what they did. All that remained was prayer. So the first man raised his eyes to heaven: "Lord, give me the strength to cross this river." In a trice, God gave him huge arms and legs, and he swam across in only two hours.

Then the second man prayed, "Lord, give me what I need to cross." God gave him a rowboat, and he rowed across in only three hours.

The third was so scared he couldn't move. So in a shakey voice he prayed, "Lord, please get me across this river!" Bingo! God turned him into a woman, and she walked across the bridge in two minutes!

✝

There are times for all of us when our brains freeze and we just can't think. So we should feel a certain kinship with the paralyzed man in Mark's gospel. He desperately needed healing, in body *and* in spirit, but he was frozen in place. He couldn't get to Jesus or even see him. So his friends did for him what he couldn't do for himself: they made an opening where there was none and gently lowered him into Jesus' presence!

What a perfect model for all of us who want to be true friends. When the people around us hit a wall and feel cut off from God and from life, we can pick them up and carry them to a new "place." We can help them reclaim their future and rediscover the Lord who's been with them all the while.

God has done that for *us* more times than we can count, carrying us out of the darkness and into the light, where we can see his face and know that he'll always be there and always be for us. His unearned gift calls for a response. As Jesus said, "What you have *received* as a gift, *give* as a gift."

✝

Give *your* gift! Don't hold back. Help your neighbors find their way out of the darkness. Help them to see the bridge and to cross over it to the Lord - and to new life.

IT'S OUR DESTINY TO
MAKE A DIFFERENCE

An old man was walking along a beach at dawn, when he noticed a boy picking up starfish that had been cast ashore in a storm. The old man asked what he was doing. "Rescuing starfish," said the boy. "They'll die if I leave them here when the sun comes out."

"But there must be millions of starfish out here. How can *you* make any difference?"

The boy looked intently at the starfish in his hand and then threw it back to the safety of the sea: "I can make a difference for *this* one!"

✝

We all want to make a difference, however small. So when Jesus says, "Re-pent," that is, re-think your lives, we take a quick inventory. "I don't lie, cheat, or steal. I don't abuse my kids or kick the cat or fudge on my golf score. All in all, I'm a pretty nice person."

We *are* pretty nice, but God wants more than just "nice". He wants us to live up to the really fine gifts he's given us. And that leads us to a hard question: would the people around us be noticeably poorer if we just suddenly disappeared?

It's a hard question, but the answer will speak itself if we take a look at the people who've made a difference in *our* lives: wise people who helped us see in the dark, kind, patient people who didn't turn away when we were at our worst, people with big hearts who loved us into getting better, people with true hearts whose values took root in our souls and are still guiding our lives.

We've been shaped, enriched, and sometimes even saved by people, who crafted noble lives out of very ordinary materials and then gave us a piece of themselves. And that lays open a stunning truth: we have the power to do the same for others! We have within us gifts that are urgently needed by people within our reach. It's our destiny to make a difference, and if we suddenly disappeared, we'd be missed.

✝

Pick up your gifts and walk. Many of God's favorite people are waiting just for you. Don't let them down. Don't betray your gifts.

QUIET GIVES WISDOM A CHANCE

An elderly man had grown quite deaf and was extremely depressed, so he went to see his doctor. The doc did his best to cheer him up, but two days later he was shocked to see him with a young blond. "As you see, doc," he said, "I took your advice!"

"Good heavens, what did I tell you?"

"You said, 'Find a *hot mamma,* and be *cheerful.*'"

"No! 'You have a *heart murmur,* so be *careful.*'"

✝

We're all inclined to hear what we expect or prefer. Proofreading is a classic example: our brain fills in what it thinks *ought* to be there, and it *speeds right past* misspellings and double the's without noticing. Even our relationship with the Lord is eroded by our lack of careful attention. For example:

1) We believe that God speaks to us through *scripture.* But many of us assume we've already heard the important parts and simply ignore scripture from Sunday to Sunday. Others twist the scriptures to their own purposes, despite St Paul's warning that "even the devil can quote scripture." The bible's riches are inexhaustible,

but they're available only to those who quiet their souls and take the time to listen.

2) When we share the *Eucharist*, the opportunity to hear the Lord's voice is extraordinary. But we let all sorts of things interfere: a cell phone, a latecomer, a growling stomach. And before we know it, the privileged moment has passed, and we've heard nothing but our own inner rambling. The Lord speaks to everyone at Eucharist. But how many hear him?

3) Every day the Lord whispers to us from *deep within*, wordlessly nudging us toward what is good, reminding us of what matters, offering us comfort and healing. If we create a quiet space where his whisper can be heard, he can help us make sense of our daily life. He can help us draw wisdom from our mistakes and can lead us toward a deeper life. Everything depends on our listening.

✝

St Paul asked a famous question: "If God is *for* us, who can be *against* us?" The answer is we ourselves, if we're deaf to his voice. Let him speak to you. Listen with all your heart. Wisdom will follow, and with it peace.

YOUR MOST DAUNTING CHALLENGES CAN BE WHAT SAVES YOU

As a kindly Grandpa was reading a story to his little granddaughter, she reached up to feel his wrinkled cheek, and then felt her own and asked, "Grandpa, did God make you?"

"Yes, dear, a *long* time ago."

"Well, did he make me too?"

"Yes, but that was just a *little* while ago."

She felt both of their faces again and said, "He's getting better at it, isn't he."

✝

Just you wait, little girl!

The gospels tell us that Jesus "understood the human heart and needed no one to instruct him about it." He knew that we instinctively run from danger, which is a good thing that's saved our life many times. But he also knew that sometimes our fear of hard choices and difficult challenges leads us to forget who we are and to abandon our deepest commitments.

Avoid, evade, deny and flee: *many* do it. But *we* mustn't. As followers of Jesus, our hearts will have no peace, if we break faith with Him and with those we *say* we love. But if we embrace the challenges and hard choices that inevitably come our way, He'll help us to dig deep and to find what is best and most noble in us. He'll help us to see life more clearly and to let go of everything that narrows our heart and turns us in upon ourselves. It's a great irony that our most frightening challenges can become what saves us.

If we look closely at the people around us, we'll probably be surprised at how many of them are in the midst of a journey through daunting challenges and hurts. By refusing to turn away, they've become more than they once were: old heart wounds have been healed as they've walked *through* the flames and not just *around* them. And much useless baggage has been left at the roadside forever.

✝

The challenge to be faithful in the face of hurt and danger is an invitation to transcend our self-absorption and to grow whole in the sight of God. Don't let fear turn you away! Instead, keep the cross of our Risen Lord Jesus before you always. And know that, even in the face of death, all *will* be well. For Jesus, who walked this road himself, will be with you at every step of the way.

HE GAVE HIS LIFE SO YOU COULD MAKE A LIFE

Have you ever wondered what Jesus was thinking as he looked around the table at the Last Supper? Those twelve men were his closest friends and his chosen successors. On his left was the very bright - and very greedy - Judas, who'd just taken a bribe to betray him later that night. On the right was the big-talking Peter, who by dawn the next morning would deny even knowing him. And the rest of his friends? The whole lot would disappear the moment the "lynching party" showed up. So much for friendship!

For an ordinary man, it would have been time to call the head waiter: "Max, separate checks, please!" But Jesus was no ordinary man. He had a larger view of life and saw more in his friends than they'd ever seen in themselves. Even though he was devastated by feelings of betrayal and failure, he couldn't give up on them. He *had* to find the key that would open their hearts to a life untrammeled by timidity and self-absorption. But his hands were empty. After three years, all he had left to give was his life. So he gave it willingly, and it slowly opened their hearts. They began to see the world through God's eyes and to become new men!

Jesus' refusal to give up on his apostles is his pledge that he'll never give up on *us* - whether we're young and distracted or old and set in our ways. He gave himself on the cross, not to satisfy some ancient debt, but to draw every one of us into the embrace of our very dear Father, the embrace that *is* our lasting home.

†

Don't give up on yourself, and don't give up on your neighbors. Dare to hope. Let Jesus show you the good he sees in you. Let him guide you towards a self-transcending goodness that knows no bounds. And remember always: *he gave his life so you could find your life!*

THE ONLY WAY TO *SAVE* YOUR LIFE IS TO *SPEND* IT!

In the golden days of radio, Gracie Allen once called a repairman to fix her electric clock. "There's nothing wrong with it," he said. "You just have to plug it in."

But Gracie insisted: "I'm saving electricity, and I only plug it in when I need to know what time it is."

✝

We all love a bargain. But many so-called bargains make no sense, because the *best* things in life are *not* free! They're bought at great price. And that's Jesus' point when he said, "Unless the grain of wheat falls to the earth and dies, it remains just a tiny grain of wheat. But if it dies, it produces much fruit."

There's no middle ground for that grain of wheat. Either it risks everything and lets itself be buried in the hope of growing into something better, or it sits on the shelf, dries up, and dies anyway. The only way to *save* its life in the *long* run is to *spend* its life *now*.

Jesus lived by that truth. He loved life and invested himself in every day as if it were his last. But he didn't cling to comfortable, settled ways. He regularly stepped into unfamiliar paths to reach complete strangers who needed him. A truly good life is like that: loving what we have and being grateful for it, but always ready to let go and embrace what needs to come next.

There's a touching story about a frail little widow who had to leave her home of fifty years. As she tottered up the sidewalk of the rest home, she said, "I love my room here."

Her son was mystified: "Mom, you haven't even *seen* your room yet."

"I know," she said, "but I love it." She'd hadn't left her happiness behind - at her old home. She'd brought it with her! She'd watched Jesus all her life, and she understood that *little* deaths are part of the process of making a *big* life. Jesus had taught her not to fear them. So when it came time to die, she was ready for that final step into a place she'd never seen before, and her last words came naturally: "I'm going to love it."

✝

Don't be afraid. Open your heart to the Lord who's ready to help you let go of whatever needs to go and embrace what needs to come next. If you do that, you'll have a fruitful life, and you'll always bring your happiness with you.

ARE YOU WORTH DYING FOR? JESUS THOUGHT SO!

The juxtaposition of the two gospels of Palm and Passion Sunday under-scores with brutal clarity a stunning reversal: Jesus was acclaimed as a hero and then executed as a heretic - all within hours. The thoughtless ease with which the crowd turned on him raises a stark question: were they really worth dying for? Why didn't Jesus just make a swift about-face and go home to a happy life with his family?

The question becomes even more poignant when we look at the cynicism and fecklessness of our own day - and even of our own lives. Are *we* worth dying for? Though it may be hard to see why, Jesus thought we are. For he could see in us a faint yet real reflection of the goodness of God - a good-ness that could grow. And none of the thoughtlessness and narcissism of his generation - or of ours - could deter him from pouring his whole self into giving us a chance at a real life.

How could he bring himself to do that? It's truly a mystery which only those who love deeply will ever begin to understand. We can only give thanks and let our gratitude flower into love that lasts.

HE HAS LONG TERM PLANS FOR YOU

A little girl named Cindy had a grandpa like no other, and she loved him dearly. He told amazing stories that made her laugh. He listened to her and explained things in words she could understand. Sometimes they'd watch the sands of his hourglass, as they fell one by one till none was left. And he'd tell her it was a reminder, that life is precious and passes quickly.

Then one day Cindy's mom told her that grandpa was sick and had only a few more days to live. "It's like the hourglass," mom said. "The sands finally run out."

"Let's go see grandpa," said Cindy. "I need to take him a present!" She found a box, put her present inside, and before long was standing at grandpa's bedside. He wasn't very strong anymore and had to struggle with the wrapping. But when he finally got it open, his tired old face lit up, and his eyes filled with happy tears: his little girl had brought him a whole boxful of sand!

She knew that, for all of us, the sands *do* run out. But her little box of sand said, "Don't be afraid, grandpa! There's more to come. God has *long* term plans for you."

†

That's what God is saying to *you* this very day: "I have *long* term plans for *you!* And if you'll walk with me, I'll help you build a heart so good and so true, that it will last forever."

Say "yes" to him with all your heart, and never be afraid again.

HAVE YOU NOTICED THE HINTS OF GOD'S PRESENCE?

An elderly couple invited a new neighbor to dinner. As they talked, the guest was touched by the old man's tender way of speaking to his wife: honey, darling, sweetheart. "It's wonderful," he said, "how, after 70 years, you still use such sweet names."

The old man blushed. "To tell the truth," he said, "about ten years ago, I forgot her name."

†

That old man is you and me. We forget half of what we learn. And we learn only half of what we could, especially when it comes to God:

– Why did God make us?

– What does he think of us now that we're here?

– And when it's all over, why would he want to raise us from the dead?

We don't know. And it may seem that we're doomed never to know. But that's not true, because God has filled the world with hints of who he is and what he's about. Take a look at the beauty of a violet, the tiny face of a child, the view of the earth from the moon, the steadying hand of a friend. All of it shouts: God is good! He's here! And, for some strange reason, he loves us!

But just in case we didn't get that message, God gave us Jesus: God-With-Us, God-For-Us! He became one of us, to show us how to *be* God's family, how to make a life that *is* a life.

✝

The Spirit of Jesus is alive within you now, wordlessly drawing you toward Life, pulling you back from darkness. Trust the Spirit. Let it lead you into the light. Though your journey may be long, the Spirit will be with you at every step, for you are cherished, as if you were the only person who ever lived!

SOMETIMES FEAR IS A GIFT

A lawyer was trying to help a widow whose husband had died suddenly without a will: "Did your husband have any last words?"

She shouted as she recalled his words: "Don't you try to scare me! You couldn't hit the side of a barn with that thing!'"

✝

Fear could have saved him, but arrogance got in the way.

Fear is one of our most powerful emotions. Sometimes it's a friend, sometimes an enemy. In seconds, it can snatch us from danger. But just as swiftly, it can make us run from what we need to face. It can freeze us in place, when we need to act - just as it did to the apostles.

Yet, sometimes fear can be a life-changing friend. That's because even the best of us resist looking at where our bad choices are taking us. We minimize, temporize, and hope for the best. But eventually reality breaks through, usually by accident. Maybe it's just another spousal fight, but this time with words that can't be taken back. Maybe it's a well-earned heart attack that says, "You're probably dying." Maybe it's the police saying your spoiled Harvard-bound son is a drug dealer!

Whatever the specifics, when ugly reality finally sinks in, it feels like the end of the world. That's when fear takes command and speaks words you know are true: "You're on the edge of an abyss. Unless you act decisively, you'll destroy what you hold most dear and waste the only life you'll ever have."

That honest voice of fear deep within you is a gift from God. It breaks into your consciousness and insists that you hear Jesus: "You have a life-or-death choice to make," he says. "Don't run away. My strength will be your strength. Together we'll take that first step in a new direction, and then another, and another. Slowly the path will reveal itself, and I will help you build anew what you almost lost."

†

Trust Our Lord. Take his hand, and let his goodness guide you through your storms and into his peace.

DON'T GIVE IN TO THE URGE TO GIVE UP

A truck driver was behaving oddly. At every traffic light, he'd jump out, beat on the side of his truck, then hop back in, until he got to the next light. A driver in the next lane was puzzled, so he rolled down his window and asked what was going on. "Well, it's like this," said the trucker. "I have a two-ton truck, but I'm carrying four tons of canaries. So I have to keep two tons of them in the air all the time!"

†

Sometimes our life can seem like a whole truckload of canaries! We break a leg. The IRS calls, our kids get in trouble, the routines of daily life grind us down, and we dream of escaping. But try as we may, we can't crawl out of our own skin. So how do we keep going?

Jesus showed us - one last time - in the final hours of his life. As he prayed in the Garden of Olives, he was so stressed by what he knew was coming, that he literally sweat blood! He could have just slipped away, but he remembered what his life was about. And a few hours later, he *gave* his life for us, not grudgingly, but willingly.

How did he do that? He did it for love, that powerful bond with his father and with us, which had been growing deep within him all his life. Love gave him the *reason* to give his life away and gave him the *courage* to do it. Love made the impossible possible!

And so it can be for us. We can keep going, keep stepping forward, even amidst the worst of times, if our love has grown so large that we've stopped counting the cost. We simply do what's needed, not grudgingly, but willingly. We see that in parents' smiling sacrifices for their children and in spouses' tender care for their helpless partners. The old wedding prayer said it well: "Love can make it possible; perfect love can make it a joy."

That's the secret that Jesus came to teach us. Live it with all your heart, and his joy will be yours!

YOUR HURT MAY BE OFFERING YOU A GIFT

A billionaire stocked his pool with alligators and announced, "If anyone can swim the length of this pool, I'll give him his choice of my art collection, the presidency of my company, or my daughter's hand in marriage." Within seconds, there was a loud splash and a frantic churning as a young man dashed the length of the pool and jumped to safety.

The billionaire was thrilled. "So what's it to be," he asked, "the art, the presidency, or my daughter?"

"Forget that!" said the young man. "I want to know who pushed me!

†

The perennial question: whom can we blame? Sometimes it's ourselves, and we learn - once again - that bad choices have bad consequences. But as often as not, nobody's to blame. An earthquake, a collapsing vertebra, a dear friend's death: some bad things just happen. We struggle to understand: are we being punished for something? But most of our answers are wrong.

Jesus gave us a metaphor that can bring us closer to an understanding. "I am the vine," he said, "and you are the branches." What bond could be closer? God feels our hurts! And he has no desire to see us suffer - no desire to punish us or to teach us a lesson. When life wounds us, it's not an "act of God," just the laws of nature following their inexorable course. God's only desire is to help us draw some good from a hurt that he did not send.

[handwritten: How do I stand in my hurts... this being the case, how to let go of resentment & blessing gracefully. How do I purify those blessings]

But wherever hurts come from, they can have an important side effect: they can awaken us to something that's not right inside us. After a humiliating defeat, we may get a first look at our oversized ego. And after our house burns down, we may realize that we've grown far too dependent on our possessions. If we face whatever gets indirectly revealed in this way, the shock of self-recognition can open our heart to the Lord, who's been waiting for us. And with his help, we can be transformed.

†

Every life has many "little deaths," but through them all, the risen Jesus is with us, reassuring us that he's conquered death, not just for himself, but for us all. Keep your eyes on him. Let him help you complete your real life's work: to be at one - with him, with his people, and within yourself. You've paid a huge price in hurt, so make sure you don't miss the payoff!

[handwritten notes: too dependent — for the place of my + gifts, energy & to my abilities (5&/d... but I did stretch & add to more whole — Be transformed into a more whole.]

[handwritten notes: God's work of two — Be a + of the Holy Spirit — trust discerning and ... gentleness spirit comb ... self control & curiosity & strength & compassion]

THE ONLY TREASURE YOU CAN ALWAYS TAKE WITH YOU

If you've ever listened closely to a flock of geese flying in a "V" formation, you've heard the whisper of their wings beating in unison. It's the secret of their strength: the lead goose cuts a swath through the air's resistance, and creates lift for the birds behind it. And so it goes through the whole formation: those out front give a lift to those who follow. The tired ones fan out to the edges, and when they're rested, they surge back to the point of the V to pull the flock along. Each takes its turn. If one grows sick, a stronger one follows it to a resting place, till it's ready to fly again.

Sticking together, taking turns at giving one another a lift, and leaving no one behind, they keep going till everyone is safely home. God surely did leave his fingerprint on those geese.

✝

In diverse ways, Jesus' teaching puts into words the lesson the geese have been living for 1000s of years: if we want love that lasts, we have to stop being afraid that there'll be nothing left of us if we give ourselves away. In fact, just the opposite is true.

Faithful love doesn't hold back and doesn't count the cost. Of course, it also gets hurt, and grows tired, and gets its heart broken. (Think of Jesus on the cross!) But it's the only love that bears lasting fruit, for as it holds to course despite the winds and waves, it changes the hearts of those who give it and the hearts of those who receive it.

So don't be afraid when life presses you to the very limits of your endurance. Love that has learned to be faithful is exceedingly strong. It will not falter or fade. And it's the one treasure you can take into the next life, for it's not just carry-on baggage, but a part of the very fabric of your soul.

✝

May the love you *give* and the love you *receive* transform your soul and bring you safely home to the One who's been watching over you, since that long-ago day when your journey first began.

ARE *YOU* GOOD NEWS?

In accord with ancient monastic traditions, a newly-arrived novice was assigned to copying ancient texts. But before long he went to the abbot with a grave concern: "We're copying from copies of copies, and we're bound to be multiplying serious errors."

The abbot was alarmed, so he hastened to the underground vault to compare the original texts with their copies. He was gone for many hours, until finally a senior monk found him crumpled face down over a manuscript, weeping inconsolably.

"Father Abbot, what's wrong?" asked the monk.

With a shaky voice the old man replied, "The word was 'celebrate'!"

✝

Sometimes the world just caves in upon us. And so it was with the apostles on the day of Jesus' Ascension. His parting command - to carry the Good News to all the world - filled them with dread. It wouldn't be enough just to *tell* the Good News. They'd have to *become* good news: *think* like Jesus and *be* like Jesus. It was utterly beyond them, especially without Jesus nearby. So in desperation they did what they should have done long ago. They laid aside their fears and gave themselves into God's hands. And ever so slowly, they became new men, ready to carry Jesus to the ends of the earth.

Like the apostles, we have been called to be Christ-bearers, not by *talking about* Jesus, but by *being like* him. But as with them, fear gets in the way. "It's just too hard," we say, "and I'm too weak - or too old." And so our soul dries up and our life becomes a tiresome replay of a "B" movie. Jesus was surely right: "Fear *is* useless!"

There's only one road out of fear, and that is trust of the One who gave us life. It's a leap into the hands of Someone we cannot see. But it's not a totally blind leap, for God has left his fingerprints all over his creation - even inside our own souls. And they tell us that he is good, and he wants what's good for us.

✝

Dare to trust him. Listen to his voice, and act on what you hear. The desert regions of your soul will spring to life. And the good news, which you'll become, will cause those around you to take heart - just as you've hoped for so long!

RECEIVE WHAT GOD IS TRYING TO GIVE YOU

The first Ascension Day *began* with solemn *words*: Jesus' command to "go out to all the world..." But it *ended* in deafening *silence:* Jesus was gone, and his disciples would never hear his voice again. With a profound sense of abandonment, they withdrew into the *silence* of their broken hearts.

serenity - Ma -and

†

Real silence is more than just the absence of noise, of barking dogs, blaring music, and whining children. Real silence is ~~something~~ *a space* we *make:* a calm opening in the mind and the heart, that allows us to hear and understand ourselves and to hear the hearts of others. In silence, new ideas are born and acquire depth; we see with greater clarity what we have and what we need; and we're able to put it into words. Real silence lets us hear voices we've not heard before. *(is an opening or portal)*

So it was for the disciples in those long days after Jesus' ascension. Haltingly, not knowing where they were headed, they created a hitherto unknown space, a silence in which they could begin to hear and draw strength from the Spirit - who'd always been there. Their description of the moment when it all came together is unforgettable: the inward rush of a mighty wind, the hovering tongues of fire, the feeling that, in the words of the early church, they'd been "kissed by God." They were no longer

In "Ma" the empty boundary provides a place for everyone's version of reality. & imagination to exist.

abandoned children. They had the Spirit's own power to "go out to all the world..." And out they went that very day.

And so must it be for us. The Spirit has been with us since first we drew breath, but despite the passage of years, we've been mostly deaf to the Spirit and immune to its gifts. And we've known much sadness because of that.

†

It's time to ~~make the move urged upon us at Confirmation~~ so long ago: *Receive* the Holy Spirit! Deep within your soul, create a silent listening place where you can hear the Spirit, who speaks with the concern of a devoted mentor. That habit of listening will change your life, and bring you joy - even in ~~sad~~ times.
difficult

* Silence is the universal Refuge - Thoreau
the pause btw musical notes
the white between letters on a page that convey
   meanings not just smudges of ink

It is the gap where the spirit can enter
it is the space for the Holy Spirit

___

what isn't - more allows for everyones
story to co-exist. It is the boundaries
of space that allows us & all of our ideas +
(openness)
exist side by side

When edges touch they have to reconcile their
common border. With the presence of a gap, space is left to
mediate btw the 2, to ... ...

BE NOT AFRAID!

A group of scientists sent a message to God: "We can now cure almost every disease. We can destroy the world and rebuild it better. We can even clone human beings. So, God, we think it's time for you to retire."

"I see," said God. "But before I go, what about a contest, a man-making contest? If you win, I'll retire - no hard feelings. We'll do it the way I did it in the old days. We'll start with dirt."

"Fine," said the head scientist, bending down to grab a handful of dirt.

"No, no, no!" said God. "*You* have to make your *own* dirt!"

✝

The world that God has made is vast beyond our imagining, but the part of it that we actually see and inhabit from day to day is very small: our home, our place of work, a few miles of road, the mall.

Our seeming mastery of that tiny space can deceive us into thinking we're masters of the universe, beholden to none - until trouble strikes, and we're shocked to see that we're just visitors here, short-term residents, and not owners at all.

Such a rude awakening is inevitable, if we forget the One who *gave* us life. But when reality finally breaks through and despair at our foolishness threatens to envelope us, we remember his words: "Would a mother forget the child of her womb? Even if she should forget, *I* will never forget you."

✝

Remember the One who loves you so much that he gave you Jesus. Marvel at that gift, give thanks, and even as you blush at your repeated mistakes, remember the words he spoke so often: *Be not afraid!*

LET HIM BE YOUR COMPANION FOR THE JOURNEY

A Baptist minister was organizing a massive revival in Moscow. His translator was struggling with American idioms, but the minister reassured him: "This is *God's* work. *He'll* make it right!" And with that he began his sermon: "I'm just tickled to death to be here."

And then came the translation: "Scratch me till I die."

✝

Life is like that: we have the best of intentions, and then they get lost in the translation. God knows that about us. He knows it will take us a lifetime of trial and error to get our lives right. And even then we'll need his help to finish. That's why he gave us the Eucharist, not as a reward for being good, but as a help for getting better. As Jesus said, "Healthy people don't need a doctor. Sick people do!"

The first Christians understood this. They called the Eucharist "food for pilgrims" and "medicine for sick people." And that's what it is: help for struggling people like us, who'll die if they don't get food and medicine for their souls.

✝

Take Jesus to your heart. Let him walk with you as only a best friend can do. He'll pick you up when you fall and pull you back when you wander. He'll stick with you through every step of your journey, and he'll be at your side when at last you hear our Father's wonderful words: "Welcome home my child!"

YOU HAVE GOOD REASON TO SMILE DEEP IN YOUR SOUL

Even a casual reader of history will note unmistakable patterns that have persisted across the ages:

—   elders denounce the young as lazy and irresponsible, while the young denounce their elders as brain dead;

—   religious leaders lament the imminent drowning of civilization in a sea of sin;

—   plagues, tsunamis, earthquakes and volcanoes come and go at will;

—   and everyone watches nervously for the next Attila the Hun, Hitler, or Bin Laden. There's always one more on the way.

✝

Jesus saw *all* of that. But he saw something *more* in the hearts of those who came to him: a desperate longing for goodness and joy, which drove them to reach beyond themselves. He said it was like a tiny seed struggling to find a place to be born. And he gave it a name, "the kingdom of God" - echoes of the loving presence of God waiting and waiting.

Whether *we've* named it or not, we've all *experienced* that lonely longing, the sense that something more true and more complete is just over the horizon. It's the invisible Spirit of God, beckoning us to ~~Himself,~~ to a new way of living that will transform us and even transcend the power of death.

God has been calling us from deep within, since consciousness first dawned in our forbears countless millenia ago. And in the fullness of time, Jesus came, God-With-Us. He *showed* us the face of God and *offered* us God's hand.

✝

Look into Jesus' face. Take his hand, and let him guide you to our Father and to the people whose love you were made to share. Take his hand, and even when hurt is near, know that you have good reason to smile deep in your soul.

IS FEAR DEFINING YOUR LIFE? BETTER CHECK YOUR GOD-CONNECTION!

A woman with five small children decided it would be nice to begin their summer vacation with planting a garden. So she took all five to a nursery where they squabbled over who got to push the shopping cart, then insisted on seeing every plant in the ten-acre greenhouse, then cried because there were no pink petunias, and finally broke a very large pot. Home at last, she sighed to her husband, "All I want is a little peace and quiet and some pretty flowers."

"Honey," he said gently, "I believe they call that a funeral."

✝

For those of us who aren't quite dead yet, peace and quiet and pretty flowers aren't on the menu most days. What *is* on the menu for all of us is a lifelong diet of things we haven't done before. It starts early and just keeps going: I haven't gone to sleep without a night light before. I haven't had to look for a job before, or been really poor before. I haven't been really old or widowed or had cancer before.

We each have our own story, and it keeps changing! But the *big* question is always the same: as the next door opens and we come face to face with our next challenge, will we freeze and pull back, or will we walk through the door and come to grips with whatever we find there?

The answer we give to that question will come from the very core of our relationship with the Lord. If we've grown close by spending regular time with him, we'll *know* we're not walking alone, and we'll take seriously the gifts he's put in our hands. There'll be no danger of our succumbing to the "living death" that fear inflicts on its victims. Instead, with peaceful hearts, we'll take hold of our gifts and step into the unknown.

✝

Spend some time with the Lord every day. Let him help you see the world as he sees it. As his wisdom and goodness take hold of your heart, his peace will be yours, and fear will have no hold on you anymore.

FEAR IS USELESS. WHAT'S NEEDED IS TRUST

A man with five young-adult offspring put a revealing message on his answering machine:

- "If you need money, press one.

- If you're in turmoil over a broken romance, press two.

- If you're being treated unfairly and wish to vent your anger on your parents, press three.

- If your car needs immediate repair or replacement, press four.

- If you're calling to inquire about our health or just to say hello, please check the number you intended to dial!"

✝

Life eventually beats up on everyone - even kind-hearted dads.

The gospels tell us that Jesus once accompanied a synagogue official to the bedside of his little girl who was very ill. But on the way they were met by someone from the house who said, "She's dead! Nothing can change that; so don't waste your time."

Those words should sound familiar, because at times we've all spoken them deep in our hearts: "it's over, and nothing can change that." We've let disappointment and fear of further pain kill our hopes, shrink our expectations, and blind us to life's possibilities.

But Jesus wasn't turned away so easily. "Fear is useless," he said. "What's needed is trust. The child isn't dead; she's only asleep."

He was speaking to *us* as well, reassuring us that the parts of us that *seem* dead and beyond help aren't dead at all. They're just asleep. But the Lord can awaken them and give them a second chance, if only we'll work with him - if only we'll let go of our fears and let his life flow into us and raise us up.

✝

No matter how hurt you may be at times, or how bad you may feel, or how often you've been in that same spot before, never turn your back on his offer of another chance. Don't miss all the good things he still has in mind for you. Take his hand, and step forward into life.

Ordinary 14 - B
Mark 6:1-6

STOP, LOOK, AND LISTEN!

A man went to a wise old monk in search of wisdom, and the monk agreed to help him. "As your first step," he said, "go outside, stretch out your arms, tilt back your head, and wait for me." And so he did. But the very moment he tilted back his head, it began to rain and didn't stop.

Hours later, the monk returned: "So have you been enlightened today?"

"Are you serious?" said the man "I've been standing here for hours, with my head up in the rain and feeling like a fool!"

"Ah," said the monk. "For the first day, that's *remarkable* wisdom."

✝

We're *all* fools. Some of us just haven't noticed it yet! That was the problem with Jesus' old neighbors. They thought they knew it all: "What can *Jesus* tell *us*?" So they continued to grind through their stale religious routines, never gladdened by his Good News, and never growing whole. It happens too often.

In the beatitudes, Jesus said, "Blessed are they who *know* they are poor." If there's ever to be any joy or truth in us or any *real* room for God and his people, we have to let go of our *need* to be right, our reluctance to listen, and our fear of being seen as the flawed, foolish creatures we are.

We can rid ourselves of all that useless baggage, if we follow a simple formula: *STOP, LOOK, AND LISTEN.*

- STOP pontificating, denying, and blaming.

- LOOK within and laugh.

- LISTEN to God and his people.

✝

STOP, LOOK, AND LISTEN. And remember that dropping your mask and laughing at yourself is an act of hope, not despair. It says, "I may be a fool at times, but I'm going to get better, because I'm *listening:* to God, and to the good people he's given me as friends!

HOW GOOD A LISTENER ARE YOU?

A woman was waiting at the airport for her college-age daughter, who was returning from a year of adventure overseas. She smiled proudly as her beautiful girl stepped out off the jetway. But directly behind her was a tall, dark man, clad only in feathers, beads and a loincloth. "Mom," said the girl, "this is my new husband!"

As she fainted, the mother moaned, "I told you to marry a *rich* doctor, not a *witch* doctor!"

†

Why is it that we so frequently get only half the message? Why do we *take in* so little of the wisdom and insight, which the indwelling Spirit and the *lived* wisdom of his people offer us every day? The answer is embarrassing: our *chronic inattention* screens out much of that wisdom, and *unexamined half truths* block out most of the rest.

(Our heads are full of those!)

All of this dawns on us when something out of the ordinary jars us awake: "Why didn't I see this before?" Only then do we realize that the Lord and his people have been with us, prompting us all along, but we've been turned in upon ourselves, fretting about life and lamenting how hard it is to walk alone.

If we don't want mental sleep-walking to impoverish the *rest* of our lives, we *need* to learn the *habit* of listening to the Lord *and* to the hearts of his good people - not so much what they *say*, but what they *are*. If we learn to live that way, we'll *know* the difference between a rich doctor and a witch doctor. We'll *know* which paths lead to life - and which do not. And we'll get a little better - and a little happier - every day.

✝

Learn to listen *with your heart;* and then give thanks that you're not walking alone anymore.

IF YOU ARE FAR FROM YOUR OWN SELF, HOW CAN YOU DRAW NEAR TO GOD?

Two little boys were attending their first wedding when one asked, "How many women can a man marry?"

"Sixteen," said his friend.

"How do you know that?" asked the other with a frown.

"Easy, just add up what the priest said: 'four better, four worse, four richer, four poorer.' That's sixteen!"

†

Even the thought is stressful! But *whatever* road we follow in life, stress is a constant companion. There's never been a time when we human beings *weren't* wrestling dinosaurs or rush-hour traffic, global famine or nuclear meltdown, Attila the Hun or Matilda the nun. The overload numbs our minds, and we're stretched so thin that we barely know who we are.

Jesus knew all the signs, and when the apostles returned from their missionary journey, he saw it in their faces. "Come away by yourselves," he said, "and rest awhile." What he had in mind was more than a temporary escape. He wanted them to *reclaim their center*, to remember what they were about and to feel glad about it - for they were about good things. He wanted them to remember that there's a Pole Star imbedded in the soul of every one of us, the Holy Spirit, to protect us from losing our way.

St Augustine understood what Jesus had in mind: "Descend into yourself," he said. "Go to that hidden apartment of your mind. *If you are far from your own self, how can you draw near to God?*" If our center is fragmented, what kind of friends, spouses or parents can we be? How can we choose wisely and live kindly if there's no calm place within us? We can't!

As William Penn said more than 300 years ago, "Step home, within yourself, and be still. Wait upon God and feel God's good presence." In the quiet, he will help you reclaim that calm place within, where there *seemed* to be only darkness, or storms, or worst of all, nothingness.

✝

The Spirit awaits you there - in calm and light. Go to him and discover anew what a wonderful gift life is.

GOD GAVE US HANDS AND HEARTS FOR REACHING OUT

The survivors of a devastating war were clearing the rubble from their bombed out church. As they gathered up fragments of long-cherished statues, they found the statue of Jesus in perfect condition - except for the hands, which had been blown away. With tender care, they placed Jesus back on his altar, and with a wisdom learned from the anguish of war, they added a comforting word from the Lord: "*Your* hands are *my* hands."

†

It was Jesus' message from the very beginning: "Give me your hands and your hearts, and together we'll build God's kingdom." We see it in the gospel about Jesus' feeding the 5000: the crowd was hungry and had no food. The apostles' solution was to send them home; but a little boy stepped forward with two small fish and some tiny loaves. It wasn't much, but in Jesus' hands it was enough. The impossible became possible, because a little boy understood Jesus' message and gave what he had.

We all know how it feels to fall short. We know the pain of struggling with what seems impossible. It's part of being human, but our story doesn't have to end there. For God wants even the smallest of our gifts to grow large. He wants us to know the joy of breaking out of dead ends and doing the impossible.

To make that happen, *we have to give him something to work with:* we have to entrust our very *selves* into his hands. That means opening our hearts, letting him show us the way, holding nothing back, and stepping forward, even when we can't see the road ahead.

Much of what life asks of us is impossible *if* we choose to work alone. But we don't *have* to work alone. *God gave us hands and hearts that are made for reaching out* to one another, for sharing burdens, carrying the weak, and healing the wounded.

✝

Open the hands and the heart that God gave you, and let *your* hands be *his* hands.

THE BIG LIE: I DON'T NEED YOU

Two cowboys were talking about a local gunman: "He's a tough dude, and he can shoot before his pistol even clears the holster."

"Wow," said the other. "What's his name?"

"Well, most folks call him Footless Frankie!"

†

Not a day passes without our seeing people "shooting themselves in the foot," destroying their best hopes and prospects. It's especially true in our friendships. People who could build wonderful lives together fall for the illusion that friends are disposable and try to go it alone.

Think of all the places around the world where generation after generation have been saying to their own neighbors and fellow countrymen, "We don't need you. We can dispose of you and make a good life for ourselves." It's a world-class illusion, but people fall for it, destroying all possibility of a good life, not only for their neighbors but for themselves, generation after generation.

But the madness isn't limited to distant spots across the sea. Statistics on violent crime confirm that the majority of victims are not strangers but friends and family members. And, still closer to home, most of the real damage to hearts and spirits happens, not at the hands of strangers, but in the family. In every case, whether far or near, the illusion is the same: "I don't need you or your help, and you have no claim on me. You are usable and disposable." What a perfect recipe for self-destruction!

But no matter how often we've fallen for it, our hearts continue to tell us quite insistently, "It's a lie!" Our hearts thirst for something quite different: for friendship, for real family that heals and doesn't harm, for communion, for a place of peace where no one need be afraid, and finally, for God. Our own deep hunger helps us to feel the hunger in our neighbor's heart, and it tells us to lend a hand, to walk together, to share the gifts we bear, and to become coaches, not critics.

†

So listen to your heart. God is speaking to you there. Build the family for which you hunger. Build the holy communion for which he made us all.

"BE STILL, REST WITH ME AWHILE, AND WAIT"

A banquet honoring a local dignitary had already stretched through a dozen speeches and four musical selections when the MC announced, "We now come to our final speaker. I'd love to give him the eloquent introduction he deserves, but given the lateness of the hour, we don't want to deprive him of a single moment of his allotted time. So I say simply, Judge Smith will now give his address."

After some weary applause, the judge rose, scanned the crowd, and then intoned solemnly: "My address is 2416 Lewis Street. Thank you very much, and good night." The crowd cheered.

✝

There comes a point when we all have to say "e-nough!"

That's what happened to the prophet Elijah. In a bold face-down, he confronted the evil Queen Jezebel before a huge crowd, and he showed how hollow she was and how phony her religion. He won the debate, but within minutes her soldiers were out with orders to kill him.

Elijah fled to the desert, wondering if winning was such a good idea: He had no friends, no place to hide, not even food or water. He had no options left, and after running for days he was so tired that he said, "Lord, just let me die," and fell asleep. But when he awakened, food had mysteriously appeared. He ate, slept again, found more food, and discovered he had the strength to make his way to safety - and to begin again.

Elijah's story should sound familiar, because there's not one of us who hasn't been brought low, defeated, and left with what seemed to be empty hands: The fifth grader humiliated and doomed by math; the mom worn to a frazzle by kids she loves; the disappointed spouse who can see no hope this side of the grave. We can feel the anguish, because part of it is our own. "I'm finished," the voices say, "too tired to hope, too tired to cry. Just let me die."

And what is the Lord's answer? He doesn't say, "Be strong!" for he knows when our strength is spent and we are empty. Instead, he says, "Be still. I am God; rest with me awhile, and wait. As a slow rain fills an empty upturned cup," he says, "I will fill you, if you hold up your cup, and wait, and be still."

✝

Remember this when life has drained you dry, and your cup is empty. Be still and wait with him. He will give you what you need to finish your journey.

OUR CHRONIC INATTENTION LEAVES US WITH LIVES WE'D NEVER CHOOSE

An ancient soothsayer lived on a remote mountaintop in Tibet. He was reputedly the wisest man in the world, and so it came as no surprise when a dying billionaire clawed his way up that snow-capped peak to pose an urgent question: "Tell me, oh great seer, what is the secret of a long life?"

The wise man sat with his eyes closed, not moving a muscle. Finally, in a barely audible whisper, he replied: "Try...to keep...breathing."

†

Real wisdom has always been in short supply. If you doubt it, track your conversations for a day, or listen to the meandering jabber that runs in your head. A large part of it is about *other* people's mistakes: "What was he thinking? How could she be such a fool?" we ask, rolling our eyes, shaking our heads, and all the while giving ourselves yet another free pass.

Our chronic inattention to the core of life, the things we need to work on, often leaves us with lives we don't like and would never choose. Too many of us are perpetually sad, because we don't see all the good that's within our reach. Too many of our marriages are wasting away because we rarely give them a second thought - except to complain. Too many of our children are headed toward a sad adulthood, because nobody's listening to their hearts. There's nothing inevitable about any of this. We *have* the power to write better endings to our stories, but that takes time and sustained attention - and it's rarely convenient.

A wise man once said, "We *can't* cure the world of sorrow; but we *can* choose to live in joy." It starts with listening to our sorely divided hearts and remembering that we can't draw near to God, if we're far away from our own selves. Choosing to live in joy means never giving up on life, even when we're old, and tired, and set in our ways.

†

Don't miss your life. Pay attention to every moment as it comes, and give it your all. *In the end, a life well and kindly lived is the only real thanks you can ever speak to God.*

HE WILL ALWAYS BE ENOUGH FOR US

A jogger spotted a tiny sparrow lying on its back in the middle of the road. He bent over for a closer look and asked, "Why are you lying there with your feet in the air?"

"I heard the sky's going to fall today," said the bird.

The man laughed, "Do you really think your spindly legs can hold up that big sky?"

"One does what one can," whispered the sparrow.

†

That's the challenge of every day of our lives. Troubles show up and we need to deal: a summer cold, a leaky faucet, a paper cut - irritants not tragedies. But lurking in the shadows are troubles of a different sort, megaton events - betrayal, financial ruin, mortal illness, which leave us wounded, helpless, and fearing for our future.

Will we find a way to carry on, to begin again? Or will we cave in upon ourselves and virtually cease to be? It all depends on *where* we've planted our roots and *how deep* they run. If our deepest roots are in our possessions - not just our property and checkbooks, but our health, our minds, our standing the community. All of them will eventually betray us, for they simply don't have and they can't give us what we really need: love, wisdom, purpose and courage. For those, our roots must run far deeper, to the very Source of Life.

Long ago, when many of Jesus' followers were deserting him, he asked Peter, "Are you going to leave me too?" Peter's poignant reply speaks for us all: "To whom shall I go?" he said. "*You* have the words of everlasting life!"

And there we have the key to our life's work: learning to put down ever-deeper roots in the One who gave us life, and remembering that, whatever comes, He will be enough for us. Like that little sparrow, we'll learn to face the enormity of life and not be afraid. For we've learned from pondering Jesus on the cross that our very dear Father will always give us the courage to do love's work and not to turn away.

THERE'S NO SUBSTITUTE FOR AN EXAMINED LIFE

A man was in a pub having a beer when he heard someone say, "Nice shirt!" He looked around, but saw no one and went back to his beer. A little later someone said, "Great tie!" This time he looked around really fast, but still nobody. "Hey, bartender. You talkin' to me?"

"No way," said the bartender. "It mustta been the peanuts. You know, they're complimentary."

✝

A little nonsense can be a healthy release, but it doesn't work as a way of life. It's what happened to the Pharisees, who were the most spiritually intense of all the Jews. As children, for example, they were taught the elaborate, seven-step, hand-washing ritual; but they never learned that it was about cleansing the heart, not the hands. All their lives they washed and washed with faithful exactitude but achieved precisely nothing. And so it went with much of their religious practice: faithful routines but no results.

Our ability to create stable routines for low-level chores, like folding the laundry or mowing the lawn, is a blessing that frees our minds for more interesting and creative work. Likewise, routine religious practices, such as favorite daily prayers, can enrich our life without much exertion. But in both cases, our routines *can* betray us. The problem is inertia: a thing in motion tends to stay in motion. A routine may cease to "work," but there's a good chance we won't notice. I once drove all the way across town to a house where our family hadn't lived for many months, and I didn't "wake up" until I turned the last corner!

That's why there's no substitute for an examined life - on every level. Most of us have religious routines and devotions that can be traced back to childhood. They can be comforting and sustaining, but sometimes, a careful scrutiny will tell us that they have nothing more to give us, and it's time to move on and go deeper.

So how *do* we go deeper? We can begin by taking time to remember that we're in the holy presence of God and then to let that presence sink in. With the help of a slow and thoughtful reading of scripture - perhaps just a verse or two, we can enhance our ability to see the world through God's eyes and to avoid the self-deception and self-absorption that are constant hazards for us all. We can engage the realities of our life in ways that make a difference: probing our successes and failures, and learning what to think of them and where to "put" them. We can get better!

✝

An examined life, lived consciously in the presence of the Lord, is the greatest gift you can ever give yourself. Don't let inertia steal that precious gift from *you!*

IS FEAR DRIVING YOUR LIFE?

A young man was taking his new son for his first outing in a stroller. The infant was screaming, but the dad was whispering calmly, "Easy now, Donald. Just keep calm, Donald. Don't be afraid, Donald. It's gonna be all right, Donald."

Nearby an older woman nodded and smiled: "You certainly know how to talk to an upset child - quietly and gently." Then she leaned over the stroller and cooed, "What seems to be the trouble, Donald?"

"Ma'am," said the father, "I'm afraid you misunderstand. He's Henry. I'm Donald!"

✝

Fear is a wily trickster, never far away, and always whispering lies:

- "If you apologize, you'll just look weak."

- "If you share, you won't have enough for yourself."

- "If you dare to love, you'll surely get hurt."

Sometimes we *can't hear* what we *need* to hear, because we're afraid it will destroy us. And sometimes we *can't say* what *need*s to be said, because we're afraid people will hate us.

Fear is the great destroyer of communion. It's sees enemies around every corner; it chokes the natural instincts to love and to share; it imprisons us inside our own heads. That's why Jesus' healing of the deaf mute grabs our attention, for he too was a prisoner, cut off from life and love. Jesus set him free, because his heart was true. And so it can be for us, if we ask honestly.

✝

Begin by *naming* your fears and *claiming* them as your own. Then place them gently in Jesus' wounded hands; rest there with him awhile.

Let his hands tell you that courage is not the absence of fear, but the willingness to go forward anyway, because you love.

His love can become your love, and you can step forward despite your fears, for he's shown you how, and he'll be with you always.

IF YOU REALLY WANT A LIFE, GIVE YOUR LIFE AWAY

A young couple was standing at the altar, waiting to pronounce their vows. The bride was trembling, the groom was pale, and both had forgotten everything they'd practiced at the rehearsal. Finally the priest asked the big question: "Do you, James, take Heather to be your lawful wife?"

With a shaky voice the groom stammered, "I, I do???"

"Nice try, young man," said the priest. "Now, could you try it without the question mark?"

✝

The goal of every human being is communion: coming together with others and helping one another to thrive. It's what we all want, but as the saying goes, "if wishes were horses, beggars would ride." A "yes" followed by a question mark will never reach its goal. Jesus put it this way: "Whoever tries to *save* his life (hoard or keep it for oneself) will *lose* it. But whoever loses (expends) his life for my sake and for the gospel will save it."

Our minds wander endlessly, and social commentators tell us that our attention span is growing shorter by the decade. But even those of us who have to struggle to stay focused can recall moments, when we connected intensely and wholeheartedly with someone we valued. As we listened and talked, it was as if the rest of the world just fell away. We forgot about ourselves, our troubles, our schedule. And for just a little while, we gave ourselves to the other and didn't count the cost. Later, as we looked back, we sensed that something inside us had changed just a bit: there was more to us, because we'd given ourselves away.

We can repeat that experience in every part of life, if we give ourselves wholly into the present, focusing on the other, holding nothing back, refusing to distract, and letting all that is secondary fall away. We'll find, to our astonishment, that as we give ourselves away, there's more to us, not less. And there's a new joy and peacefulness in our soul.

✝

Learn to live wholeheartedly in the present. It's the most valuable life-skill you'll ever develop. Your life will grow larger and richer in ways you never would have dreamed.

JESUS CAME TO SERVE, NOT TO BE SERVED. WHY DID *YOU* COME?

A man was feeling poorly, so he went to his doctor for a check-up. "I have bad news," said the doctor. "You don't have long to live."

The man was shocked: "How long have I got?"

"Ten," said the doctor shaking his head.

"Ten? Ten what? Months? Weeks?"

The doctor interrupted: "Nine...eight..."

✝

We're no strangers to tragedies, but there are few things more distressing than watching people of talent betray their gifts. We sense there's something missing at their center, and all that's left is an array of fragments - some quite fine - that just don't add up.

Thomas Jefferson is a classic example. He was a brilliant defender of the rights of man, but he cheated every man he ever did business with. He denounced slavery all his life, but never freed his own slaves - not even in his will. He was treated like a son by George Washington, who made him Secretary of State. But in return, he secretly used government money to fund vicious newspaper attacks on Washington. He beguiled and fascinated people and then used them mercilessly.

Observing that kind of tragedy is akin to having a bad meal and wondering how something so unpleasant could have come from such good ingredients. Upon reflection, the answer speaks itself: this is what happens when people make themselves the center of the universe.

If our life is only about us, there'll be a void at our very center. The kindness, courage, understanding, balance and fairness, which could have given coherence and integrity to our hearts, will never develop, because the center of our being is stunted by self-absorption. And we'll never be more than a jumble of disconnected parts that never add up to anything of lasting worth.

✝

Jesus showed us a better way: "If you want to be first of all," he said, "become the servant of all." Be grateful for your gifts and invest them in your neighbors for the long term, as Jesus did. Not only will your neighbors thrive, but all the parts of you will grow and come together in a coherent whole that really does make sense. True peace will be yours, and the heart you've made will shine brightly into eternity.

HAS THE HABIT OF THINKING SMALL SNEAKED UP ON YOU?

A new mom had twins, and the doctor told her to make sure they got an hour's sunshine every day. So every day she put the little boy out in the sun from twelve to one o'clock and the little girl out from one to two. The doctor was puzzled: "Why don't you just put them out together?"

"Well," she said, "I just wanted to make sure they'd each get the *full* benefit of the sun!"

✝

Thinking small is an ancient habit. It was old news in Moses' day, when the official prophets got in trouble by letting the Spirit speak directly to the people at the center of the camp, instead of keeping the Spirit under wraps in the prophecy tent. They hadn't yet learned that "the Spirit blows where it will."

Something similar happened in Sunday's gospel. Outsiders were healing people in Jesus' name, which outraged the apostles. "Jesus," they said, "if you don't stop them, we'll lose control!"

And so it continues in our own day:

- we could build up God's family, but we build walls and gates, thinking small.

- we could change the world, but we go along to get along, thinking small.

- we could probe the mysteries of life, but we live by cliches, thinking small

- we could be rich with friends, but we obsess about the risks, thinking small.

†

This life of ours is an extraordinary gift, full of possibilities. But it's more than just a dress rehearsal. *It's our one-time path to eternity.* So give it your full attention. Think big. And love big. The Spirit will be with you at every step of the way.

FRIENDSHIP IS A FRAGILE BRIDGE

A startling notice appeared in a local newspaper: "Readers of our new book, *SKYDIVING MADE EASY*, should note the error on page 12, line 3. The words *'state zip code' should* read *'pull rip cord.'* We regret any inconvenience."

✝

Life can be exceedingly inconvenient at times, especially when it comes to our friendships [relationships], those special bridges we build to one another. They may be special, but they collapse with regularity, because we're such careless builders. We rarely ask:

1) Why am I building *this* bridge, to *this* person?

2) Who is it for? Us? Or just them [me?], or just me?

3) Can it bear the weight of two-way traffic?

4) Is it grounded in something solid? and respectful

Even if we've pondered all that, there's still a good chance that our bridges won't last, because the glue that could hold everything together, an understanding [tolerant] heart, is missing. Such a heart is not the work of a day. It's the result of slowly getting to know our real selves through and through, of seeing our selfishness and ~~cruelty~~ *judgmentalness*, and knowing sadly that there's more yet to come. That *could* lead to despair, but for those who listen with a humble heart, it's an invitation to receive God's forgiveness *& mercy* so deep within, that we finally let go of our shame and learn to forgive *ourselves*. And the other side of that same coin, we finally stop condemning others and start forgiving them, as generously as we have *been* forgiven.

At last we'll have the heart *& minds* to build bridges that will endure. When we look at one another, we'll see more than rag bags of sins and mistakes; we'll see fellow pilgrims trying to find their way and needing the same help and understanding that we so sorely need.

The challenge will never be over. Our friends will get tired, cranky, and dis-spirited, and so will we. They'll make mistakes, paint themselves into corners, get confused and even forget our names, and so will we. Only an understanding heart with its habit of boundless forgiveness *& mercy* will save our bridges from collapsing under their own weight.

✝

Let the Lord help you grow such a heart, and become a master bridge builder for his big family. You'll never walk alone again.

DON'T LET THE GOOD
LIFE DEVOUR YOU!

There's a species of jellyfish that has a taste for a particular variety of tiny snails. It devours them with ease, but then discovers that their hard shells are indigestible. The snails attach themselves to the walls of the jellyfish stomach and begin to eat their host! By the time they grow to maturity, the jellyfish is no more. The diner became the dinner, consumed by what it consumed!

†

Jesus repeatedly warned us about this: we can be consumed by what we consume. In our hearts, we *know* what makes a life worthwhile: building good bridges, sharing our gifts, searching for truth and *being* true. We *know* that, but our attention wanders. We become hummingbirds, frantically searching for a sweeter blossom, always in motion, never staying long. That can end in only one place: disappointment and an empty heart.

The only humane alternative is to attend to each part of life *as it unfolds,* and to accept the hard truth that every day requires many choices of us, that every choice is a tradeoff, and that every "yes" requires *many* "noes."

To say "yes" to helping a child with homework is to say "no" to a glass of wine with a friend. To say "yes" to preparing a sermon, is to say "no" to the intriguing novel that beckons nearby. Good choices don't come easily, because we cherish the illusion that our choices don't add up. But they always do.

So where do we find the wisdom to avoid being devoured by the good life? Where do we find the strength to say the "yeses" and the "noes" that *need* to be said, and then the strength to follow through, once we've given our word? Jesus tells us that our Father will help us *find* that strength, if we stay close to him.

✝

From deep in your heart, ask for the strength you need, and *you'll find it as you need it*. You'll be *able* to speak the "yeses" and "noes" that need to be spoken. You'll be *able* to keep your word. And the Lord's peace will be yours.

JESUS KNEW WHAT *REAL* POWER IS

A few years ago, a group of job-hunting Harvard seniors was given an interesting choice. They could settle for $50,000 a year, with the proviso that their *friends* would get only $25,000. Or they could have $100,000, while their *friends* got $200,000. To the surprise of their interviewers, most of those savvy grads took the first option: *half* the salary, so long as *they* got *more* than their friends! Their need to be number one trumped everything.

†

Several of Jesus' apostles were bitten by the same bug and made cheeky requests for top spots in his new kingdom. They'd done nothing worthy of note, but that didn't stop them from wanting power. It's a very human problem, on the playground, in faculty meetings, in the board room. We *like* to call the shots and to be top dog, but in the long term, it's not enough to make a life. And it's dangerous as well, almost always deteriorating into a *need to dominate* that can take us down some very *bad* roads.

Jesus understood that. *He* knew that *real* power - power that lasts, isn't about controlling people or bending them to our will. It's about setting them free, giving them hope, and helping them to find the courage for great deeds. Think about the good people who've stretched your vision and taught you to hope. They gave you a part of themselves, which lives on *in you* to this very day. That's *real* power, but it was never about them, just about you.

Saint Pope John 23rd was once asked why he convoked the Vatican Council. He replied simply: "Because I wanted to make people's lives a little less sad." And he did just that, by gently setting aside the things that didn't matter, and instead, showing us Jesus. Pope John was old and sick, and he lasted barely four years as pope. But he showed us Jesus in ways we'll never forget. He became a part of us, and even now the memory of his goodness brings us healing.

✝

What greater power could any of us hope for? To enliven, to hearten, to make people's lives a little less sad by showing them Jesus. Let that vision capture your heart and never let it go.

ARE *YOU* BRAVE ENOUGH TO LOOK?

A woman who was quite advanced in years, was still living in her own house and taking good care of it. She was particularly proud of having replaced all her windows with double-pane glass. But then her contractor called: "Lady, it's been a whole year since we installed your new windows, and you still haven't paid for them!"

"Now look here, young man," replied. "Just because I'm a senior citizen doesn't mean I'm stupid! Your salesman gave me a guarantee, and I'm going to hold you to it. I remember his exact words. 'In just one year,' he said, 'these windows will pay for themselves.'"

✝

Tough lady! Not too clear, but tough.

Mark's gospel tells us about a young man who was tough, and brave as well. He was blind and he wanted to see, but not just the birds, bees, and flowers, and the faces of his friends. He wanted to see the *inside* of things, which was risky, because like all of us, he had some serious things to look at: Was there any point to his life? Did he have anything worth sharing? Could he get back on track after the wrong turns he'd made? Was it too late to build a life? Is love worth all the risks and hurts? He had lots of serious stuff to look at.

Many people spend all their lives in the dark, because they're afraid to see. But that blind man stepped boldly into the light, because he knew that Jesus was right: the truth can set us free.

The truth about all of us is simultaneously horrifying and exhilarating: we've sinned early and often, *but* God has given us the power and the opportunity to grow and to change. No matter how late it is, we can make a better life.

✝

Trust that and open your soul to the Spirit of Jesus who dwells within you. Whisper the words of the blind man: "I'm *ready* to see. And I'm *not* afraid. For the One who helps me to see will also gave me the heart to do whatever is needed to grow into his likeness."

Ordinary 31-B
Mark 12:28-34

IS LOVING WITHOUT COUNTING *YOUR* HEART'S FIRST INSTINCT?

A congregation was struggling to build a new church. Almost everyone had stepped forward, but there was one major holdout, the town banker, who claimed he was in desperate financial straits: "My son's Ivy League school tuition is $40,000. My mother's in a rest home at $60,000 a year. My daughter's husband abandoned her and their nine children, and she needs $50,000 a year. How can I possibly say "yes" to the church, when I've already said "no" to all of them?"

✝

That story calls to mind a recent book, *The Righteous Mind,* which argues persuasively that most of us make up our minds almost instantly and only later try to find reasons or excuses. That's because our "thinking" almost always starts with a deeply-held idea or value, whose power sweeps us toward a swift decision. But what often follows is an extended struggle to save face and to make sense of what will never make any sense at all.

That banker's refusal to help build a new church is a perfect example.

His determination to maintain his extravagant lifestyle despite its consequences for his family made his heartless decisions easy. What took some time was fabricating a plausible excuse - and sometimes there just isn't one!

So what are the core values that almost instantaneously dictate *our* decisions? Our culture has a ready supply: winning, having the best, keeping safe, never getting caught. They're all seductive, and they've got plenty of glamorous cousins as well, but none of them can deliver the long-term satisfaction they promise. Even when they're dressed up in our cleverest rationalizations, they have no staying power.

Jesus told us that there's only one way of looking at life that will *always* lead to good decisions and a peaceful heart. The great commandment: "Love God with your whole heart, your whole soul and your whole mind, and love your neighbor as yourself." In sum, love without counting!

✝

Let that vision take hold of your heart and shape your every move. If you do, there'll be no need of excuses or second thoughts. Your life will speak for itself; and your soul will find rest.

LET LOVE WORK IT'S
MAGIC ON YOUR HEART

A little girl was gravely ill and desperately needed a transfusion of a rare blood type. Her little brother shared the same type, but he was only five and was terrified of doctors. Yet when his parents explained that his sister would die without his special blood, he held out his arm: "take mine!"

When the procedure was completed, the parents were stunned when they heard their boy whisper: "Mommy, *when do I die?*" He thought that in giving his blood, he was giving his life away too. But he did it anyway!

✝

Where does that kind of love come from? That's the same question posed by two stories from scripture: one widow gave her last bit of food to a total stranger, while another dropped her last penny in the poor box. Where *does* that kind of love come from? It comes from *being* loved - and *knowing* it. For with that knowing comes a thankfulness that *draws us forward to complete the circle of love.*

It's so natural. Why don't we experience it more often? The problem is our old nemesis, our habitual inattention: we just don't notice how deeply the Lord and his people love us. The kindness, goodness and beauty, which fill our lives, come to us so quietly and so regularly - as if on schedule! - that we rarely find our hearts moved with joy as they were *made* to do.

†

Take the time to *receive* the signs of love that surround you every day. Let them touch your heart, and fill you with wonder, and propel you to complete the circle of love again and again - never counting, always giving thanks.

Ordinary 33-B
Mark 12:24-32

WILL YOU BE READY WHEN THE FUTURE BECOMES THE PRESENT?

A mother mouse was scurrying across the kitchen floor with her six little ones, when all of a sudden she came eyeball-to-eyeball with a very large, very mean cat. She was terrified but stood tall, squared her shoulders, and roared at the top of her lungs, "Bow-wow!"

In the blink of an eye the cat was gone, headed for a safer neighborhood. Meanwhile, mother mouse gathered her little ones and explained: "I've always told you how important it is to learn a second language!"

†

For a moment, her life seemed to be over, but it wasn't. It happens to us all: a tragic loss, a fatal illness, a dreadful failure, and then the chilling question: what now? What do we *do* when the sky falls in?

What we do depends on what's been going on in our minds and hearts as the years have been racing by. Like all of creation, we exist *in* God, who is the very ground of our being. Scripture tells us that he holds us in the palm of his hand and shelters us in the shadow of his wings. But have we taken that to heart? Have we formed a conscious bond with the One "*in* whom we live, and move, and have our being?"

If we have, and the bond is deep, we'll be able to see *through* the confusion and the pain when trouble strikes. Deep inside we'll *know* that, despite all appearances, God is still with us and for us, and his fatherly love will carry us through *whatever* may come, even death itself.

✝

Stay close to him, never turn away. When at last the lights grow dim, and the night draws near, and your world fades away, you'll see him face to face, and you'll know who he is!

HE HAS GIVEN HIS WORD, AND HE WON'T TAKE IT BACK!

Several times each century, for more than a thousand years, Westminster Abbey has served as the site of the ancient liturgy for the coronation of England's kings and queens. Vested in gold with a sword encrusted with diamonds at his side, and bedecked with gold rings and bracelets dripping with rubies and sapphires, the new monarch receives the golden orb and the scepter - one for each hand. And finally, the crown, studded with priceless gems, is placed on his head to the sound of trumpets, choir and organ, as he is seated on his royal throne.

We've all seen the pictures and been dazzled by the ancient trappings of monarchy. But we've probably missed the core of the ceremony, a simple act, which has its roots in the Old Testament, in King David's time. The king is anointed with holy oil: head, heart and hands. And by that symbolic act he's bonded to his people for the rest of his days, as their protector and guide.

†

For Israel, and later for England, things rarely worked out quite that nicely. But it was that *ideal* of a king's unbreakable bond to his people that led Jesus to call himself a king, for his commitment to us is total and irrevocable. It has no escape clause, as his crucifixion revealed so clearly!

In giving us his undying pledge, Jesus also gave us a model for the whole of our lives: standing by one another steadfastly, even when the journey grows long and difficult. Our natural instinct is to flee inconvenience, discomfort and pain. But as we've learned, that can only leave us empty handed. Only faithful love, on the good days and the bad, will bring us to the rich, full life that is our destiny.

†

Walk with your neighbors, as faithfully as Jesus walks with you. Bring your very best - head, heart, and hands - to every moment. And never give up. As the days and years pass, your heart will tell you that you've made the right choice.

CYCLE C

IT ALL DEPENDS ON HOW YOU
ARRANGE YOUR MIND

A frail woman of 92 was delivered to a nursing home in a cab. She'd recently lost her husband of 70 years, and she'd come to the nursing home because she couldn't live on her own any longer. After waiting in the lobby for two hours, she was still smiling when the nurse guided her along a corridor, telling her about the tiny room that would be her home. "I love it," she said with the enthusiasm of a school girl.

"But, Mrs Jones, you haven't even seen the room yet," said the nurse.

"That has nothing to do with it. Happiness is something I decide on ahead of time. Whether I like my room or not doesn't depend on how the furniture's arranged. *It's how I arrange my mind.* Each day is a gift, and as long as my eyes open, I'll remember that and be glad."

✝

Terrible troubles are a constant across history: Vesuvius erupts, Krakatoa erupts, Mount St Helens erupts. Attila the Hun attacks, Genghis Kahn attacks, Hitler attacks. The Black Death kills, polio kills, AIDS kills. Troubles are with us always, but they have power over us only to the extent that we give it them. We can let them define our lives, or we can listen to the Spirit who whispers from within, "I am with you always, and I'll give you the heart to face even the worst of days."

God doesn't promise to hold us harmless as the volcanoes erupt, the warriors rage, and plagues run their course. But he does promise that, whatever our troubles, the very core of us, that which makes us who we are, will survive and not be destroyed.

✝

Cherish God's daily gift of life and of fatherly love, and even amidst life's troubles, be glad, every day, to the very end.

WHAT ARE YOU ALLOWING TO DEFINE YOUR WORLD?

"...Prepare the way of the Lord. Every valley shall be filled in and every mountain shall be made low." Isaiah the Prophet 40:3

✝

A little boy wouldn't stop fighting with his sister, even though his parents warned him: "Santa's watching!" So they took him to *see* Santa, who bent over and whispered to him sternly: "There'll be no presents for boys who fight with their sisters!"

Afterwards, his dad asked, "What did Santa say?"

The boy responded blithely: "He won't be bringing any toys to my sister!"

✝

Young or old, we all have to struggle to keep a solid grip on reality. As we stumble through life, repeating the same old mistakes, it doesn't take long to despair and to feel trapped in a lifeless valley where the sun will never shine. In every age, many of God's people, even little children, live and die alone in such dark places.

Equally isolated from life and love are those whose self-absorption persuades them that they're the center of the universe, better than all the rest and needful of no one. They dwell in the imagined majesty of grand mountaintops, only to discover too late that they're empty and alone and have no one to turn to.

Those dark valleys and frozen mountaintops, and all the other barren and loveless places that we make for ourselves, have no truth in them and no life. But even in their darkness, Jesus whispers to us the truth that can change everything: God is our loving father, always at our side, tending our wounds, wiping away our tears, so we can see his face.

✝

Take heart; and take his hand. Let his truth set you free from all the dark and frozen places in your soul. Let him show you where the *fullness* of life is *still* waiting for *you*.

HE HOLDS YOU IN THE
PALM OF HIS HAND

In his autobiography, Pope John 23rd admitted that it took him a while to get used to being pope. When a tough problem came along, he'd say, "I need to talk to the pope about this." Then he'd remember with a start: "But *I'm* the pope!"

On the night before the opening of the council, he was so worried that he couldn't sleep. "Giovanni," he finally said to himself, "Is it the pope who guides the church or the Holy Spirit? Eh, Giovanni, it's the Holy Spirit. Go to sleep!"

✝

At any given moment, there are all sorts of worries, large and small, lurking in the shadows of our minds, waiting to steal our joy. Countless "what-if's" seize our imaginations and terrify us about things that may never happen. Memories of past mistakes steal our confidence and dash our hopes for the future.

None of it makes any sense, if we *believe* what we *say* about God holding us in the palm of his hand. If we really *do* believe that, we shouldn't be such easy prey to worry and fear. Confidence and joy should be the hallmarks of our lives. And gratitude for the love that fills our lives should impel us to share what we *have* and what we *are* without any expectation of return - not just on Christmas, but every day of our lives.

There's a great paradox in all this, for as we give ourselves away, we become more, not less. St Francis understood: "It is in giving, that we receive. It is in pardoning, that we are pardoned. And it is in dying - our final gift of ourselves to God - that we are born to eternal life."

✝

Don't be afraid. Give thanks and rejoice always, for the Lord has already given you what you need. If you listen closely, your heart will whisper your next step, for that's where the Holy Spirit lives all your life long.

TOO MANY OF US WALK ALONE

A monkey and a hyena were walking through the forest, when the hyena complained, "Every time I come this way, a lion jumps out and beats up on me."

"I'll go with you," said the monkey, "and be on *your* side."

But when the lion pounced as usual, the monkey just watched from the safety of a tall tree. "Why didn't you do something?" moaned the hyena.

"Well," said the monkey, "you were laughing so hard, I thought you were winning!"

†

Our hearts have many desires, but none as deep as the desire for a friend, someone to walk with us on this long journey. Yet the hard truth is that too many of us walk alone. Too many of us fight the lions and carry life's burdens alone, even in the midst of a crowd.

That seemed to be the destiny of the Virgin Mary's cousin Elizabeth, who'd never given birth to a single child across a lifetime of longing. In her very old age, the rooms of her little house were silent, not cheered by the laughter of the many grandchildren who ought to have been there.

Elizabeth had listened to God's promises since earliest childhood: "I will never forget you, never abandon you. Don't be afraid." But with the passing of the years, it had become harder to hope, and she'd begun to wonder if those words of scripture were really true or just the wishful thinking of some ancient scribe.

But then one day she heard Mary's voice at her door, and sensed the presence of God's Holy One. And in her weary and wrinkled body, she felt the quickening of a new life. The Lord had been with her all along, and all his words were true!

✝

There's never been a time when God wasn't stretching out his hand and beckoning to *you*. Don't hesitate! Take his hand and hold it tight. The lions *will* come. They always do. But you won't be facing them alone anymore.

HE CAME TO STAY

A busy mother was making pancakes for her two little boys, who immediately began to fight about who'd get the first one. So she decided to teach them a lesson about Christian behavior: "Boys, if Jesus were here, he'd say, 'Let my brother have the first pancake. I can wait.'"

With that, the older boy turned to his little brother and said, "Mikee, you can be Jesus!"

✝

That's why God gave us Jesus: because we *needed* him to show us what a *really good* life looks like - from the very beginning to the very end. And we *needed* him to help us find the heart and the determination to become like him, *despite ourselves.*

When Jesus was born, the angels called him Emmanuel: God-With-Us, God who'll never leave us, God who has the power to heal us and to be our strength no matter what comes.

✝

Let him light your darkness and warm your coldness. Let him wipe away your tears, so you can see his face. Then take his hand, and walk with him all the way home. He knows the way!

Holy Family - C
Luke 2:41-52

IF YOU WANT YOUR FAMILY TO WORK, ANCHOR YOUR LIFE IN THE LORD

A mother of four small children was trying to get everything ready for a major family gathering on Christmas Eve. She was barking orders like a drill sergeant: "Put away your toys! Don't get your clothes dirty! No, you can't have any more!" And so on.

The four-year-old was underfoot, so she was sent to the living room to play with the Nativity set. Before long, she was having a make-believe conversation with the three kings, and this is what her mother overheard: "I don't care who you are; get those camels out of my living room!"

✝

Being family is hard work, and the Holy Family was no exception. As with us, their only hope was to anchor the lives firmly in the Lord.

And that's what we see them doing as they took serious time out to make the three day journey to Jerusalem. They knew that they needed to drink deeply from the *source* of wisdom and strength, if they were ever to be what they so urgently wanted to be for one another.

The gospel says that Jesus progressed steadily in wisdom, age and grace. That didn't just happen. It was the result of a whole family working together with God as their partner. They couldn't read the future any more than we

226

can. All they had was an exceptional attentiveness to the present, which is where the Spirit dwells. And step by step they made their way into the future to which God was calling them.

The road they walked is the same one we travel. Will we find *our* way as they did? It all depends on where our souls are anchored. The Spirit is as near as your own breath - and never silent. Are you listening?

Epiphany - C
Luke 2:1-12

IF YOU WANT TO *FIND* THE LORD, YOU HAVE TO *LOOK* FOR HIM

A man was complaining about his job: "The stress is killing me!" he said. "I have migraines, I can't sleep, and I just found I have an ulcer. If I don't quit, I'm headed straight for a heart attack!"

"So why *don't* you quit?" asked his friend.

"Well," said his pal. "They have this great health plan!"

†

Making sense of life isn't easy. It's a serious quest, but there's always something else demanding our immediate attention, and we only too gladly leave the hard thinking for another day. Yet deep inside, nagging questions keep bubbling to the surface and won't be silenced: Is there any point to all our striving, or is this just a long, painful journey to nowhere?

That's how life seems to many who, by sheer inertia, have settled into a spirituality that's the equivalent of painting by numbers: lots of paint, but no soul. No wonder so many wander away from their churches: they know Jesus' *name*, but they don't know *him*. It leaves a terrible empty place in their souls, and it hurts.

The wise men in the Christmas story knew that hurt, but they didn't just settle for it. They sensed there was more to God than just a vague cloud somewhere on the fringes of the universe, so they invested themselves in a lifelong search to find God. And when the mysterious star appeared, their quest took on new urgency. They left home and hearth and risked everything to find the One from whom all life flows. And they would not be deterred.

At the end of their long journey, they were astonished to find God with a human face, lying in a manger. It wasn't what they'd expected, but they were able to recognize him, because they had listening hearts. Jesus spoke not a word, but by his fragile presence in that lonely stable, he let their hearts know, that we don't walk alone. God is with us at every step, and all of His creation is slowly moving to that far off point, where all will be one in Him.

✝

Don't settle for a sterile inner life. Look into the face of Jesus - in the manger or on the cross - and see the One who is closer to you than your own breath. Embrace him, receive His strength and His goodness, and bid farewell to all those ancient fears.

HE CHOSE TO BE OUR BROTHER

A little girl had a serious question: "Mommy, if the end of the world came and everybody was getting ready to die..."

Mommy braced herself: "What now?!

"Mommy, if the end of the world were coming, would you have to take back your library books?"

†

In her own naive way, she was trying to get a grip on life: where do I fit in this big world? Jesus himself wrestled with that question for a long time: where are my gifts leading me? What *is* my life's work? When at last the answer became clear, he did something that *seems* to make no sense: he asked to be baptized. What was that about? He had no sins!

The breathtaking realization, which had finally seized him, was that God was calling him to be brother to us all, to walk shoulder to shoulder with us, to the very end of our journey. And he said "Yes!" with all his heart, stepping down into the Jordan to be washed in the *common* waters, silently declaring himself our brother for life - and beyond.

Great commitments like that can be dangerous, as the rest of Jesus' life made so clear. But there's something even more dangerous than *making* serious commitments, and that is *dodging* them, thinking we can build a life without risk or sacrifice, or without any fire in our soul. It's an illusion. The reality is: No sacrifice, no love. No love, no joy.

✝

Quiet your soul and listen to life with an open heart. You'll hear the Spirit of Jesus. And in him you'll find the courage to speak a "yes," that will last until your work is truly done and you come to rest in the hands of God.

DON'T LET SELF-ABSORPTION BLOCK YOUR PATH TO JOY

A strange procession was entering a cemetery: two hearses, a woman in black with a pit bull, and finally 200 women in single file. "What's going on here?" asked a bystander.

"The first hearse is for my husband," said the woman in black. "My dog killed him."

"And the second hearse?"

"My mother-in-law tried to save him, but the dog got her too."

The bystander was definitely interested: "May I borrow your dog?"

"Sure," said the widow. "Just get in line."

✝

We all crave happiness. It's in our DNA. So why are we so unhappy so much of the time? Because we keep investing our hearts in things that have nothing of enduring value to give us in return. For the woman in black, revenge looked like bliss, but soon enough the taste of victory would sour, as it had for so many before her. The old reliable tricksters, fame, fortune, power, and controlled substances, continue to seduce a goodly share of *every* generation with their long-discredited promises. On and on it goes. Why are we such easy prey? Because we live on the run and take so little time to look at *where* we're going. Before we know it, we've played all our cards, and it's time to leave.

Jesus showed us a different path. Whether it was restoring laughter to a wedding feast whose wine had run dry, or preventing the murder of a woman caught in the act of adultery, or comforting his grieving friends - "I will be with you always!" - as he disappeared into the clouds, his heart was always listening and doing just what was needed. Step by step, he gave us the formula for happiness that lasts.

True happiness comes only to hearts that are open and listening, devoid of pretension, and ready to share life without counting the cost. Happiness comes to those who understand that life is not just about *them*. It's about *all of us together*, going forward shoulder to shoulder, leaving no one behind and no one outside the circle of our love.

†

Let that be the measure of your every deed. Happiness will follow.

HAS YOUR LIFE BECOME
AN EXTENDED NAP?

A rumor was spreading through the Vatican that the Second Coming of Christ was about to occur. Within minutes the corridors and offices were in full panic, and the senior cardinal hastened to the pope: "Holy Father, we have reason to believe that the Jesus is about to return. What shall we do?"

The pope looked up from his papers and said, "Look'a busy!"

✝

That wouldn't be hard for *us!* Not a day passes without our being inundated with commitments that sometimes press us to the very edge. As a matter of simple survival, we've learned to devise routines that minimize the effort and attention required for many of our tasks. Our morning routine can take us from bed to Cheerios, while barely activating our brain. On Sunday morning, our car finds its way to church, and our feet lead us to our favorite pew without a moment's doubt. And it's not only action-routines that we devise, but also idea-packages for ready use without rethinking - sometimes for a lifetime!

There's a lot to be said for routines: they save time, reduce stress, and give us a sense of control in a world that so often feels out of control. But there's a downside. Our routines can work so smoothly that they lull our brains into a happy lassitude, just as our computers "go to sleep" when we let them sit idle. And that spells trouble, for as new information comes our way, our brain either misses it completely or gives a glazed look at the new data and dismisses it as "old news." If you doubt that, try to recall the last time you thought long and hard about a cherished idea, and then changed your mind.

Letting our brains go dormant touches our friendships as well, slowly eroding the bonds that hold us together. Eventually there comes a day when one or the other of us finally powers up his brain and discovers she has no idea who the other is or what he's about.

✝

Jesus came "to restore sight to the blind and to set captives free."

Let him awaken your spirit and restore your sight. Let go of the fixed ideas and routines that hold you hostage. And dare to probe the hard questions, that have been awaiting your attention for so long. Above all, stay awake, and let every day become a true journey, a joy, and an act of praise.

GOD HAS GREAT DREAMS FOR YOU!
ARE YOU DREAMING *WITH* HIM?

A man was driving his wife home from church, and the usual interrogation was under way: "Did you see those ugly plastic flowers, and Mrs O'Brien's weird hat, and that tacky couple next to us, and how unshaven the usher was?" and on and on.

The poor fellow had seen none of it, utterly confounding his wife's expectations. "John," she said, "sometimes I really wonder why you bother going to church!"

†

For good or ill, expectations change our lives, sometimes opening grand vistas and drawing us to new heights and sometimes erasing hopes and killing dreams.

Jesus saw this as he tried to help people to trust that God is kinder and more understanding than they'd imagined, and that with him, their lives could be infinitely happier than they'd ever dreamed. But as often as not, after a flash of hope, the dream was just too much for them. Their long-standing expectations of a vengeful God were like a strait jacket they couldn't escape. Jesus' Good News sounded like Chinese - totally foreign and too good to be believed. And the gospels tell us that many of them just walked away, their moment of hope drowned by a lifetime of wretched expectations.

It's a sad story and a warning. By becoming one of us, Jesus invited us to walk with him, to dream great dreams, and to build lives and loves worthy of God's children. But too often we've settled for lives that are narrow and self-absorbed. Think about those who live for gossip and whose joy is slashing and burning reputations. They steal others' lives and dare to call it living, just one of life's many tragedies of low self-expectations!

✝

God's gifts are the measure of his high hopes for you - even when the day is far advanced. Dream with him. Leave behind all that's narrow and mean. Let him help you grow into the big-hearted life that *he* can see - even now.

IF YOUR LEARN TO LISTEN, YOU'LL NEVER WALK ALONE

The captain of a transatlantic flight announced, "One of our engines has failed. But not to worry. We'll just need an extra hour."

Thirty minutes later he said, "Another engine has failed, which means two hours' delay, but we'll be fine."

Before long he was back: "A third engine has failed. The delay is now three hours, but we still have one engine."

With that, an irate passenger spoke up: "If we lose one more, we'll be up here all night!"

✝

Engines fail. And *we* fail - often. Like Peter, we say to ourselves, "I've labored all night and caught nothing." And we wonder "why"?

- Eve gave the classic non-answer: it was someone else's fault!

- Sometimes we've aimed at the wrong target and failed by sheer luck: Mr Wrong left town! But we just had to try the same mistake a few more times!

— Sometimes we chose well, labored valiantly, and then forgot where we were going.

— Sometimes we saw a goal - stop smoking or die - and wished we could stop...And then, we went on to our next wish.

All our failures had one thing in common: we tried to walk alone. And that doesn't work. God has given us brothers and sisters to share our journey, to join hands in common purpose, and to rescue one another when we're confused or lost. Without that *communion*, we'll *all* fail!

But God also gave us his own Spirit of Wisdom, ceaselessly calling to us from deep within, helping us to sustain our vision, drawing us *towards* what is true, and pulling us back from what has no life in it.

✝

Learn to be quiet and to listen to the Spirit. And learn to listen to the good people who love you so much. You'll find the wisdom to set a right course, and you'll discover you *have* the heart to see it through - because you're not walking alone.

WHAT'S *YOUR* PLAN?

An executive was determined to get rid of all slackers, so when he noticed a young man doing nothing he asked, "What's your salary?"

"$300 a week," said the young man.

With that, the CEO pulled out $1200 and growled, "Here's four weeks pay. Now get out and don't come back!"

Feeling pretty good about his first firing, he looked around the room and asked, "What did that goof-off do around here?"

Someone in the back of the room mumbled, "He was the pizza guy."

✝

Been there. Done stupid! Haven't we all!

Making our way through life's twisting paths is no easy task, and that's why most of us hatch some sort of plan that we hope will see us through. And that can spell trouble, as following make clear:

+ "I'm the greatest and nobody will ever beat me." (You bet, Saddam!)

+ "My good looks will be my salvation." (Thank you, Marilyn Monroe!)

+ "My portfolio of dot.com stocks will outlast me by decades." (Great wallpaper!)

+ "I'm a certified genius and my brain will always save me." (Welcome to assisted living!)

Most folks don't say it that clearly, but millions of us are depending on such illusions to make it through life. They don't work, indeed there's only one plan that does. It starts with the stark realization that, in the end, nothing on this planet can save us, because the core and essence of us is spirit, and we're going to live on long after the planet and everything on it have ceased to be.

When our life's work here is completed and our bodies have fallen away like the first stage of a rocket into space, what will live on is the core of us, our hearts, and cradled inside, our loves. That's why Jesus came: to help us build hearts big enough to hold many loves, the kinds of loves that last.

✝

So fix your eyes on Jesus. If you trust Him, He can help you build a heart big enough for God and his people, who will fill you full forever!

NO MORE EMPTY HUGS!

A man was hard at work at his computer, when he realized that his six-year-old was standing beside him and he asked what she needed.

"It's bedtime, Daddy. I came to say good night."

Keeping one eye on his screen, he gave her a big hug and a kiss: "Good night, sweetheart. I love you. Now off to bed."

A few minutes later, he looked up and saw that his daughter was still there. "Honey, I gave you a hug and a kiss. What do you want now?"

Maria replied softly, "Daddy, you gave me a hug and a kiss, but *you* weren't *in* it."

†

Quite so! We set out to do what Jesus would do, and too often end up with just the shell of it - the empty hug, the outside but not the inside, the unblessed hosts instead of the Eucharist. Why does this happen? In part because we have superior forgetting skills, which is why our daily prayer is so important. It's our remembering time, and without it we lose our way.

†

But there's another reason we're not as compassionate and loving as we'd like. We get confused by cheap imitations: the warm and fuzzy feelings when they play "our" song, the tears we shed at the kids' Christmas play. They're wonderful moments, but they're not love. There are lots of other love imitators: never saying "no" isn't love. Neither is keeping the peace by avoiding hard truths or running from painful reality.

True love has deep roots. It's always ready to listen, hope and forgive. Love tells the truth and lives the truth, even when it's hard. It delights in its gifts, but also delights in sharing them. Yet it knows how to say "no" as well as "yes." Reality is complex, and love understands that complexity and acts on it.

The ultimate challenge to our loving wisely and well is our lack of self-knowledge. There's only one kind of looking inward that will ever bring us *both* self-knowledge *and* a change of heart. It happens with the Lord at our side and His face before our eyes. In His presence, we can begin to see ourselves as He sees us. We can begin to see the waves we send rolling into other people's lives, and we can find the heart to change.

✝

If you truly desire to be like Him, go to Him often, be still, and listen to Him. In the presence of His powerful goodness, your heart will empty itself of all that isn't true, His light will overcome your darkness, and the energy of his love will fill your emptiness. Then at last there will be in you no more blindness, no more aching hollowness, and no more empty hugs!

THE PATTERNS DON'T LIE

A conscientious young priest desperately wanted to be a good preacher, so he asked a parishioner to listen to his homily each week and give him feedback. After mass the first Sunday the parishioner came to the sacristy and offered his judgment. "Warm," he said. "Warm!"

Now the priest was a people person so he liked this evaluation of his sermon as it continued across many months. But eventually he began to wonder: "Am I missing something here?" So he went to the dictionary and found the definition of 'warm': "Not too hot"!

✝

Poor fellow! He heard what he wanted to hear as we're all wont to do, and that's why Sunday's gospel is made for us. Jesus is asking us, "Do you know who you are on the inside?"

Our first impulse is to say, "Of course, how could I not know after all this time." But if we've learned anything from life, our answer will be more careful: "I know something of myself, but there's much that I haven't seen yet, much I need to see."

"Ah," the Lord will say then, "that means we can do business. Look past your words and wishes and good intentions," he says, "and check the patterns of your deeds. They paint a clear picture of what you're really like on the inside. Only rarely does one of your deeds fall outside those patterns."

And why is it so important to know who we are on the inside? Because we can't get better till we see where our problem is. We can't make our deeds match our words till we see the mismatch in living color. Fine words and good intentions can set up quite a smoke screen and can fool the best of us. How often have we said, "I'm just fine," and have meant it, but been dead wrong?

†

Take the time to look closely at the real patterns in your life and don't be distracted by the surface noise of idle talk, wishes, and busyness. It's a crucial step towards a truly big life. Thank God, he doesn't ask you to do this work alone. Thank God, never alone!

DON'T LET YOUR "YES" FADE INTO "NO"

Just as a man was coming out of anesthesia, he opened his eyes to mere slits and murmured to his wife, "You're wonderful!" A while later, his eyes opened a little more and he whispered to her, "You're beautiful!" An hour later, he opened his eyes wide, looked at his wife and said off-handedly, "Oh, hello."

"What happened to 'wonderful' and 'beautiful'?" she asked pointedly.

"Oh that," he said, "the anesthetic wore off."

†

Things change! "Yes" becomes "no" with chilling speed. Fears about what we may be missing keep us looking for better offers and treating our commitments as short-term parking, instead of a part of our very selves. What an irony, that in a relentless quest for more of everything, we could end up empty shells.

Jesus knew this as he searched his soul in those 40 days in the desert. He had exceptional people skills and he was ever so bright. His career options were unlimited and tempting! But instead of wealth and power, he chose a lifetime commitment to being our brother and helping us grow whole.

Even when we aren't much interested in him, he persists in reaching out to us.

Faithfulness like that can endure storms, plagues, and famines and still stand firm. If we ever hope to find peace and contentment, that's where we have to look: giving our hearts away and never taking them back. It's the work of a lifetime, but Jesus showed us the way, one step at a time.

✝

Look upon his cross. Take some time to probe the depth of his commitment to you. His cross is where you'll find the courage to make large commitments that last. And as you live them, they'll enlarge your soul, and you'll become a blessing to all whose lives you touch.

HE HAS CONQUERED
DEATH FOR US ALL

In the midst of a raging storm, a sea captain realized that his ship was going down. He asked if anyone knew how to pray. "I do," said one of the men.

"Excellent," said the captain, "you start praying, while the rest of us put on our life jackets. We're one short!"

†

Life is a gift, but at times it can be unthinkably cruel. And so it was for the apostles on their final pilgrimage to Jerusalem, when Jesus revealed the horrors of his death only days ahead. They were stricken, confused, and angry at the evil of it all. So Jesus took them to a mountain top and renewed their hopes by showing them where he was really headed: not just to death, but to the resurrection. He helped them to look *through* the pain that lay immediately ahead and to see his destiny as God's son. And it began to dawn on them that this was *their* destiny too.

They didn't want to leave that peaceful mountain top, but the work that would bring them to the resurrection was not up there. So reluctantly they descended the mountain, picked up the fabric of their lives, and made their way to Jerusalem, knowing full well what awaited them.

To each of us has been assigned a piece of God's kingdom to be helped to grow and flourish. The work is slow, and too often seems pointless or simply impossible. We grow weary and lose our way, and we hurt. But even in the darkest times, Jesus is there, calling us for just a moment to the mountain top, reminding us where we're headed, to the resurrection, and reassuring us that we do not build alone.

✝

Listen to him. Trust the vision he shares with you: he has conquered death for us all!

BECOME AN EXPERT AT SECOND CHANCES

One foggy night a ship's captain saw lights heading straight toward him. "Change your course 10 degrees south," he ordered.

But the other ship replied, "Change *your* course ten degrees north."

"I'm a captain! Change your course south."

"I'm a seaman first class. Change your course north."

The outraged captain fired back: "I'm giving you one last chance. I'm a battleship!"

The seaman's reply shut down the conversation: "I'm a lighthouse!"

✝

Too often we misread the "lighthouses" in our lives and think we're in the right and doing just fine. Not so with Jesus. As the gospel says, "he needed no one to tell him about human nature. He was well aware of what was in people's hearts." That should make us nervous.

We started sinning young: fighting over toys, hating a new sibling, manipulating the family with tantrums. With time, we developed our specialties, hurtful things that became habits, things we did without thinking. And every time we made one of those bad choices, a dose of poison headed straight for our hearts. And the results are the damaged hearts the Lord sees, when he looks within us.

So why didn't he just wash his hands of us long ago? Why was Jesus willing to die for us, when he *knew* what was in our ancestors' hearts and what *would* be in ours? Because he saw our hunger for what is good and our willingness to start over again and again, even though we know we'll often fail. And seeing that, he took us to his heart and encircled us with his compassion.

It's all gift! If we understand that, our hearts will *have* to soften, and we'll have to *give* compassion as freely as we've *received* it. It's our chance to thank God for a lifetime of second chances.

✝

Become an expert at giving second chances - not grudgingly but willingly. You'll heal many hearts, including your own, and the Lord will know that his kindness to you wasn't wasted.

WHAT WILL YOUR EPITAPH BE?

Louis Pasteur had reached the summit of his career and was ready to retire. But he was troubled by the thousands who died every year from rabies, so he struggled on in his lab in search of a cure. When a neighbor boy, little Joseph Meister, was bitten by a rabid dog, Pasteur knew that he'd die if he weren't treated. So he risked his reputation and his fortune and used his untested drug. And the boy lived! Years later, when the great man died, his heirs found amidst his papers the epitaph he wanted on his tombstone. Just three words:

Joseph Meister lived.

✝

Pasteur knew what his gifts were for: helping God's people to thrive. That's what the whole of Jesus' life taught us: we owe it to our neighbors to lead good lives, because how *we* live shapes so much of how *they* live. We can see it in families. Children ignore much of what their parents say, but they imitate what they do, their mannerisms and speech patterns, their values and habits. How often we've heard a child respond to a scolding by saying, "Well, you do it, mom!"

Young or old, we have vast power to encourage others toward goodness. Our compassion, our faithfulness to commitments, and our readiness to share and care, can make lasting impressions on the hearts of those around us. And most of the time, we don't even know that anyone is watching.

Of course, there's another side to that coin: the way we live can drag others down. Our harsh words and cruel judgments are like viruses, and so is our compulsive competition for the toys that we persuade one another that we need. Walking away from our commitments makes it easier for our friends to walk away from theirs. Just by being who we are, we can deceive others into feeling okay about what's not okay at all.

We long for a world of peace and justice, where everyone has enough and no one is left out. Take a decisive step towards building that world by giving your best self to God's family every day. You'll change more lives than you'll ever know! And what an epitaph it will make: He changed lives! She changed lives!

Lent 5-C
John 8:1-11

GIVE THE GIFT OF PEACE TO THOSE WHO'VE INJURED YOU

There's an old *Peanuts* cartoon that opens with Lucy glaring at her mother: "You promised me a birthday party, and now you say I can't have it. It's not fair!"

Her brother Linus tries to intervene: "Why don't you just say, 'I'm sorry, mother. You were right.'"

Lucy ponders that for a moment and then cries out, "I'd rather die!"

✝

How readily we let our egos back us into places we'd never want to be. And how foolishly we shut our hearts and plug our ears, when those who love us try to speak the truth that will set us free.

Jesus knew this about us, as he faced the woman who'd just been caught in the act of adultery. He hated what she'd done, but he looked into her heart, past all the foolishness and confusion, and saw there one of God's own. And he knew he had to save her - from herself as well as from her accusers.

As for her accusers, why were they so angry and so anxious to kill her? They remembered their own adulteries, and were afraid their wives might do the same thing. So she had to die, to warn their wives. But the man would go free, because "boys will be boys!"

It would have been tempting to condemn the whole lot of them, but instead Jesus spoke to the goodness and honesty buried deep in every soul: "Let the one who is without sin cast the first stone." With that he fell silent, looking at no one. And one by one, they dropped their stones and, with heads bowed in shame, walked away.

✝

Jesus' gift was not the stony silence, with which we so often assault one another, but the peaceful stillness that makes a place safe for finding the truth that can set us free. Give that gift ungrudgingly to those who've sinned against you. Give it as the Spirit has given it to you. If it has no strings attached, doors will open for them, and the light will wash their darkness away. And your own soul will be glad.

ARE YOU WORTH DYING FOR?
JESUS THOUGHT SO!

The juxtaposition of the two gospels of Palm and Passion Sunday under-scores with brutal clarity a stunning reversal: Jesus was acclaimed as a hero and then executed as a heretic - all within hours. The thoughtless ease with which the crowd turned on him raises a stark question: were they really worth dying for? Why didn't Jesus just make a swift about-face and go home to a happy life with his family?

The question becomes even more poignant when we look at the cynicism and fecklessness of our own day - and even of our own lives. Are *we* worth dying for? Though it may be hard to see why, Jesus thought we are. For he could see in us a faint yet real reflection of the goodness of God - a good-ness that could grow. And none of the thoughtlessness and narcissism of his generation - or of ours - could deter him from pouring his whole self into giving us a chance at a real life.

How could he bring himself to do that? It's truly a mystery which only those who love deeply will ever begin to understand. We can only give thanks and let our gratitude flower into love that lasts.

JESUS' RESURRECTION IS THE PROMISE OF YOUR OWN

Many years ago, the famous film director Cecil B DeMille was canoeing in Maine, when he noticed a swarm of water beetles swimming nearby. One of them crawled up the side of his canoe, but when it reached the top, it shuddered for a moment and then died. Before long, its shell turned dry and brittle in the sun. But then, as DeMille continued to watch, it split open. Something entirely new burst forth, a rainbow-colored dragonfly that soared into the sky.

The other beetles must have seen that dragonfly, but it was no kin of theirs. So they forgot about it until the surprise of their own resurrection. But DeMille didn't forget. He asked himself, "Would God do that for a beetle, but not for a human being?" In his heart he knew the answer.

†

Deep down, *our* hearts know the answer too. But life can wear us down and make us doubt: our bodies grow weak, our plans go awry, and the shortness of life is ever before us. "Is this all there *is*" we ask, "just a brief flash across the sky and then darkness forever?"

That's the fear that takes hold of us some days, but it's not the truth. Jesus' resurrection proves that for all time. After three days stone cold dead in the tomb, he was raised up by our Father to a new kind of life, beyond all the limits of time and space.

But Jesus' resurrection isn't just about him. It's the promise and the guarantee that all whose hearts are joined to him will rise and soar with him.

✝

Trust that with all your heart, and this very moment taste the beginnings of your eternity with him!

PEACE IS MORE THAN JUST QUIET

Life is a gift, but sometimes it wounds [*worries*] us grievously, and too often we *let* those wounds [*worries*] rob us of our peace. But even more destructive than our hurts are our rampant egos, the most relentless robbers of joy and peace in all the world.

[*little self important saints*]

Our (egos) are incredibly needy: they *need* to be right, [*need to control*] *need* to be the center of attention, *need* to have their own way, *need* to have more and be better than anyone else. Ego's curse is a perpetual state of anxious unrest. No wonder the words of the prophet Jeremiah resonate so deeply in our souls: "Peace, peace, but there *is* no peace."

God's will for us *is* peace, not the quiet of the grave, but the serenity that Jesus had. It's more than just the absence of trouble or hurt. It's a state of mind and heart that's so rooted in the Spirit of Jesus that our deepest desires are reshaped, our nagging neediness fades, and our fear loses its power.

As we think and feel *with* the Spirit, we'll walk through [*each day &*] the hard times peacefully, because we know we're loved, we'll delight in the joys of life, even in troubled times, and we'll be able to give ourselves away without fear of losing ourselves. [*The Holy Spirit will transform our minds so that we will know God's Peace*]

✝

That's what Jesus showed us, and that's the life we were made for. Don't let a rampant ego steal that life of peace from you!

NO PAIN IS EVER WASTED IF YOU LET IT DO ITS WORK

Sometimes our brains just slip into a fog, whether from mind-numbing fear or simple exhaustion, and we find ourselves doing unthinkable things. So it was with Peter, who in a state of acute fear denied Jesus *three* times. The memory of it tormented him later. And when the risen Jesus appeared in the upper room, Peter was stricken when he asked *three* times: "Peter, do you *really* love me?" It was pure agony, but it wasn't about punishment. It was about cleansing and healing Peter's self-inflicted wounds and getting him ready for the rest of his life.

There's a message here for all of us. Our mistakes are constant and beyond numbering, and sooner or later each one of them leaves its sad consequences on our doorstep. And alongside them are the *random* hurts and sufferings that drop out of nowhere but are as inevitable as pollen in spring. In both cases, our first instinct is to flee the pain with the help of flimsy excuses, moving vans, controlled substances, and lots and lots of plastic (which *ought* to be a controlled substance). But there's nowhere to hide - at least not for long.

So much pain. It seems pointless, but it's not. For no hurt is ever wasted, if we embrace it and let it do its work. Each has its purpose, just as Peter's agony in facing Jesus did, washing his heart clean of arrogance and self-delusion so he could *be* the solid rock his brothers needed him to be.

†

Hurts will keep coming to you until the day you die, some earned, some free of charge. Each one offers something you need for your journey, though it may be hard to see. Trust that, take it to prayer, and give it time. The truth will slowly reveal itself. What seems so pointless is often what will save you from yourself and open the door to the best part of your life.

LOOK INTO HIS FACE, HEAR HIS VOICE, AND TRUE YOUR LIFE!

A father was awakened by a violent storm, and immediately thought of his little son alone in the dark. As he ran down the hall, he heard the boy's tiny voice: "Who's there? Who's in my room?"

Dad was about to shine his flashlight on the boy, but realized that would only frighten him all the more. So he turned the light on his own face: "It's me, son. Everything's all right. Go back to sleep." And so he did: there was nothing to fear, because his father had shown him his face.

✝

In giving us Jesus, God showed us *His* face, which says, "There's a special place in my heart for you, and all I ask is that you make room in *your* hearts for your neighbors." But somehow we keep forgetting that second half of that. We delight in being loved, but instead of expanding our own circle of love, we let it shrink. Not just on the global scene but in families and neighborhoods, on the road and in restaurants. Even the best of us can act as if we're the only ones who count.

There's no remedy for this narcissism but turning back to our Good Shepherd, looking into His face, hearing His voice, and truing our hearts. His truth cuts to the very heart of things. "You'll never know peace," He says, "until you understand that life has to be shared, not hoarded. You'll never be happy until you make the circle of your love big enough to hold *whoever* comes into your life." It's not negotiable. It's just the truth.

✝

Look into His face, hear His voice, and true your life!

Easter 5 - C
Rev 21:1-5 & John 13:31-35

LET JESUS TEACH YOU THE WORDS OF A NEW SONG

Years ago Jules Pfieffer did a sad cartoon strip tracing a boy's life from pre-school to old age. It went something like this: "I worked hard in kindergarten to get into the right grammar school. Then I worked hard to get into the right high school. I worked really hard to get into an Ivy League college, and even harder to get into the best grad school. I worked very hard to get a great job, and then doubly hard to be promoted. And now, after working harder and harder for 50 years and finally becoming CEO and President, I'm retiring."

The last picture showed a shriveled old man, hunched over a walker: "But I still don't know what I want to be when I grow up!"

✝

Life is a treasure that we seldom appreciate before we've spent most of it. As the birthdays keep coming and we keep scrambling, a day can come when we feel cheated by life. What we've worked so hard to achieve can lose its luster and can seem just a handful of dust.

It's a painful moment, full of fear and confusion, but it's also a graced moment. For even as the realization dawns that we've invested too much in what can never fill our emptiness, an alternative will slowly reveal itself.

In the words of scripture, the Lord will teach us the words of a *new* song: *live* like Jesus, give life, and don't take it away.

That new song is a remarkably reliable litmus test for every relationship and for every moment of our day. It's true for parents and children, priests and scientists, soldiers and presidents. It can give an accurate answer to that most fearsome question: Who *am* I at the *core* of my soul? It can help us see what's not right in us, and it can guide us toward the good and the true.

✝

Trust that test, and act on what it tells you. If you do, the people around you will thrive, you'll find a new richness in your life, and the likeness of Jesus will begin to show itself on your face, because you've begun to *live* like him!

Give life always, and never take it away.

IS THE ROADMAP THAT JESUS SENT YOU STILL SITTING ON YOUR DESK?

In the final days of World War II, when I was just a little tyke, I loved to sit with my grandpa every day at noon, when he came in from his garden to listen to the war news. My little stool was right next to him, so I had to be very quiet. Then one day, the radio said the war was over. And I can still remember thinking with glee: peace meant no more news and no more having to be quiet!

✝

The peace never really came; it never does. So what are we to make of Jesus' promise: "My peace I *leave* you. My peace I *give* you." Where is it? Why haven't we got it? Why are we so often at war within ourselves and with those around us? The answer is painfully simple. Jesus gave us the roadmap to the only peace that lasts: love God with all your heart and your neighbor as yourself. But our attentions drift, and we let foolish preoccupations shape our lives:

— We're obsessed with imaginary needs, and then are disappointed when our wishes come true.

— Our hearts are soured by sundry angers and fears that we cling to as if they held the elixir of life.

— We bury ourselves in the routines of work and forget our loves!

266

Take a look at the patterns of *your* choices as they reveal themselves across your day. Do they make sense? Is love transforming your minutes and hours a step at a time? Will you be better tonight because you loved today?

✝

At the end of the day, those are the only questions that matter. And in your heart, you'll know the answer before you ask.

NOW IT'S YOUR TURN!

It wasn't easy to be a Catholic in the days of Elizabeth I. Priests were hunted down and so were the people who helped them. One such person was Margaret Clythrow, who was imprisoned for teaching her children catechism and then was condemned to death when a chalice and mass vestments were found in her house. The night before her execution, Margaret made an enigmatic request to her jailor: "Give my shoes to my daughter Anne." It was a quiet message from mother to daughter: "Follow in my footsteps, Anne. Carry on."

✝

That was Jesus' final message as he ascended to the Father: "I've shown you the way. Now, carry on." His words were intended for us as well, but they mean something different for each of us. It's not that we can pick and choose, as if Jesus' message were some kind of buffet. It's just that each of us has different gifts, which summon us in different directions.

The basic rule is the same for us all: give life and help people to thrive. It starts with getting a clear fix on what our gifts are (and what they're not!) and then finding where those gifts intersect with others' needs, so that we know what to bring to them and when to bring it - and when to be very quiet.

That sounds easy enough, but too often we get tangled up in our own needs and end up bringing something useless or even hurtful. Here are a few one-liners that we'd never *speak*, but might very well *act* upon:

- Hi, Dad, I'm here to run your life.

- I'd really like to help you, but right now I'm overwhelmed with my needlepoint.

- I've looked through all my closets, but there's nothing I can spare.

Each of those foolish statements is an expression of heart failure in our mission as Christians which is to grow together into God's family.

✝

Take a fresh look at your gifts, scan the horizon, and then hear Jesus say: "Follow in my footsteps." You'll see! You are very much needed, and you have plenty to give, right here and now!

IS YOUR HEART COLD? LET THE SPIRIT SET YOU ON FIRE!

A man named Sam bought a new computer and immediately ran into trouble, so he dialed for help. The expert began rattling off all sorts of jargon and Sam got totally lost. So with great humility, he said, "Could you just explain it to me slowly, as if I were a little child?"

"Sure," said the computer man, and spoke very slowly: "Son, could you please put your mommy on the phone."

✝

From our earliest childhood, God has been explaining life to us, whispering to us through the beauties of the earth, through the loves He's given to warm our hearts, and through the goodness and even heroism that He energizes within us.

And yet, we often miss his message and give in to an agonizing fear that life has no meaning. When that happens, some people just walk away from their faith, while others go through the motions, but without heart or hope. That's what the apostles did after the Ascension. They hid in the upper room, sad and bitterly certain that they'd been abandoned. But they'd got it all wrong!

What we celebrate on Pentecost is that they finally got it right. They finally took in what God had been whispering *in their hearts* since they were little kids, and what Jesus had been telling them since the first day He met them: God loves us deeply and He wants us in *His* family forever! When the apostles finally *got* that, they caught fire and carried the Good News to the ends of the earth.

Now it's our turn to lay hold of that vision and let it set us on fire: He is *in* us, *around* us, *above* us and *below* us. He is totally *beyond* us and yet is, at every moment, our partner and mentor, our comforter and guide.

✝

Receive Him into your life and you'll never be at a loss. He'll be your Today, your Tomorrow, and your Forever!

Trinity - C
John 16:12-15

YOU CAN AFFORD TO TAKE THE RISK

There was a man whose wife had a mean, scrawny, moth-eaten cat that he utterly despised. One weekend, when his wife was away, he drowned it in the dead of night and buried it deep in the backyard. When his wife returned and found that her precious pet had disappeared, she was devastated. So he offered a $10,000 reward for its safe return.

"Are you crazy?" asked his friend. "What if the cat shows up?"

He replied with a contented smile, "When you know what I know, you can afford to take the risk."

✝

Not long before he died, Jesus said, "I have much more to tell you, but you cannot bear it now..." What was he talking about? His death? No, he'd already told them about that. The end of the world? No, he'd already said he didn't know. He was talking about the dark places in our hearts, which seem so ugly and so beyond fixing that they frighten us into pretending they don't exist. It's like trying to protect ourselves from the hazards of the freeway by driving with our eyes closed.

Jesus knew this about us and told us again and again, "Don't be afraid." He assured us that we can risk opening our eyes and looking squarely at the inner darkness that has terrified us. We can afford that risk, because we know that the Holy Spirit of Jesus is guiding us through the dark one step at a time - never giving us more than we can handle, but always giving us the power to light up our darkness one room at a time.

✝

Trust the Spirit who abides with you always. Know that there is no journey into the dark that is too long or too far. "When you know what *we* know, you can afford to take the risk." Take it now!

ARE YOU RECEIVING THE LORD OR JUST THE BREAD?

A Jewish theologian was interviewing for the position of Britain's Chief Rabbi, when an arch-conservative member of the committee quoted the words of the prophet Samuel to King Saul: "'Thus says the Lord... Attack the enemy, kill men and women, infants and children, oxen and sheep, and spare no one.' Now that's in the bible," said the committeeman. "Do you *believe* God said that to Samuel or *not?*"

The rabbi answered, "I believe Samuel *heard* it, but I don't believe God *said* it!"

✝

Would that we were all so wise, but we're not. Rarely an hour passes without our saying or doing something stupid or hurtful. We stub our toes, wreck our cars, overdraw our accounts, and hurt those we love. And none of it comes as a surprise to God, who knows that growing up, at any age, is a succession of two steps forward and one step back.

When I was a little boy, my grandparents kept a record of my growth on a door frame in their kitchen. On every visit, I'd stand very tall, grandpa would mark my new height and the date, and then he'd congratulate me heartily on my progress upward.

Jesus told us that God takes that same kind of delight in *our* growing up, even when it's barely an inch at a time. And to keep us growing, he gives us the Eucharist, not because we've earned it, but because we need it to heal our wounds and keep us on course.

At the Last Supper, Jesus gave the Eucharist to all twelve of his apostles. Eleven of them drew healing and courage from that encounter with him. But for Judas it was just another piece of bread, because his treasure and his heart were elsewhere - not with Jesus.

✝

Don't follow his failed example. Plant your heart deep in Jesus and follow wherever he leads. No matter what challenges come, he'll always be your strength. He'll always be enough for you.

Ordinary 10 - C
Luke 7:11-17

DON'T TRY TO TAME THE HOLY SPIRIT

The election of a new pope is always cloaked in mystery, and only later do we piece together some clues as to how it came about. The election of Pope Francis is no exception. We've learned recently that in the conclave of 2005, Cardinal Bergoglio was a strong contender by the second ballot. But he pleaded with the cardinals to look elsewhere, because he "lacked what was needed." And so they did.

Eight years later in the days before the conclave of 2013, Cardinal Bergoglio gave multiple interviews reiterating that he should not be considered a candidate, because his "gifts lay elsewhere." And that seems to have been his state of mind as the doors of the Sistine Chapel were locked and the conclave began. Yet just 24 hours later, when the white smoke appeared and the new pope stepped onto the balcony of St Peter's, it was Cardinal Bergoglio, Pope Francis!

†

What happened in those few hours between his heartfelt protests and his landslide election? We'll never know for sure, but a few weeks later Francis gave one of his spontaneous chapel homilies which hints at an answer.

The Holy Spirit upsets us, he said, because it moves us, makes us walk, pushes us forward. We want to calm down the Spirit, even turn back the clock, and that's wrong. It's stubbornness, wanting to tame the Holy Spirit!

Resist that temptation, he said, and go with the Spirit wherever it takes you.

I suspect that Francis was giving us a peek at the profound experience that turned his "no" into "yes." He must have sensed that *he'd* been resisting the Holy Spirit. So with all his heart, he gave himself into the hands of the Spirit to be led into a future he'd never imagined and could not see.

✝

The temptation to tame the Spirit is with us always. When the Spirit beckons you to paths you've never walked before, don't be afraid, don't resist. Go with Him. He'll always be enough for you, and He'll never lead you astray.

Ordinary 11 - C
Luke 7: 36-50

CHOOSE THE REAL GOD, NOT THE VENGEFUL FRAUD

A man took a hi-tech job in the aerospace industry, and his friends wanted to know what he actually did. He tried to explain, but nobody "got" it. So he settled for a simple answer: *I'm a defense contractor,* which seemed to satisfy them. But then one of the guys asked, "What do you put up mainly - chain link?"

†

Some folks never "get" it!

Despite all their learning, most of the Pharisees never "got" Jesus' simple message. They'd seen him heal the sick, feed the hungry, comfort the sad, and forgive sinners. They'd heard him say that God is our very dear father. But they'd have none of it. For long ago they'd formed their idea of God out of the meanest parts of their own souls. And that left them trapped in a loveless place where there were only rules and more rules - and endless fear, because no rule can ever be perfectly kept.

But the sinners and prostitutes, with whom Jesus dined regularly - to the shock of the Pharisees - "got" Jesus' message, because they knew who they were, they knew their neediness, and their hearts were untouched by any illusion of their own self-sufficiency.

†

Each of us has a choice: to be a *recovering* sinner who trusts the loving Father that Jesus showed us, *or* to be a *fear-filled* sinner who'll never see our dear father, but only a hard-hearted policeman waiting to punish and condemn.

Choose the real God, not the vengeful fraud. Let his fatherly love take hold of your heart. If you do, you'll find the joy and the peace for which you were made.

THERE'S NO SUCH THING AS A LIFE THAT'S BOTH GOOD AND PAIN FREE

Many of us have a recurrent nightmare about being back in school and facing an exam, which we're about to flunk because we never went to class. We're horrified, but it's only a dream.

In real time, the apostles faced an exam by Jesus himself: "After all our time together," he said, "what do you think I'm really about?"

Peter opted for the grand answer: "You are the Christ who will come in power and glory." But Jesus just shook his head. By then they should have known that power and glory were *not* what he was about.

Jesus had a larger vision: "if you want a *real* life and not just an illusion, step outside your ego with all its self-centered ambitions and obsessive fears of failure. Give yourself into the present and the people who fill it, and don't run away when you get hurt."

There's no such thing as a life that's both good and pain free. The moment we commit ourselves to another person or to any good work, we make it inevitable that hard choices will be demanded of us: the kids will get in trouble, the spouse will die, business will turn bad, the best candidate will be rejected, the congregation will hate the sermon. Commitments are dangerous!

Long before Good Friday, Jesus saw the tragedy that was coming, but he didn't flee. For that would have given the lie to everything he'd said about love and sacrifice. Instead he *freely gave himself* into the hands of those who would kill him. He did it for a love so strong that it could prevail over the deepest fears and hurts. He understood the equation: No sacrifice, no love. No love, no joy!

✝

Don't betray God's gift of life. Dare to love God's people with all your heart. You'll be hurt again and again. But God who *is* love will fill your soul and carry you forward, as he carried Jesus to the resurrection.

Ordinary 13 - C
Luke 9:51-62

TRUST THE SPIRIT AND DON'T TRY TO TAME IT

A cowboy knew he was in trouble when a raging bull came charging straight at him. Just in time, he dived into a hole, but leaped right out again. The bull came back, madder than ever and the cowboy ducked back into the hole, only to pop out again. He did this several more times, until a stranger shouted, "Hey, man, why don't you just stay in the hole?"

The cowboy's reply was succinct: "There's a bear in there!"

✝

At times we all feel trapped by life, though, if truth be told, a good portion of our traps are of our own making: lifestyles and relationships that don't work, grudges, fears and addictions we just can't let go. And then the traps we inherit: dysfunctional families, wounds from early childhood, limited opportunities. It's a bleak picture.

But if we're paying attention, we'll hear the words of Jesus echoing across the centuries: "I've come to set you free." We'll hear him calling us by name as he called his dead friend Lazarus: "Come out of that tomb and into the light, and I'll show you what real living is."

If there's a modicum of trust in us, we'll respond to that call and step forward. But doubt and chronic forgetfulness will likely intervene before long, drawing us back to our old ways. Our story could easily end there, were it not for the Spirit, who is God's strength, alive within us, drawing us forward, never relenting, and never despairing of us.

✝

Don't try to tame the Spirit or to dilute the vision it sets before you. Give it your trust and your full attention. You'll be stretched beyond anything you ever thought possible, and you'll have doubts, but the Spirit will always be enough for you. Trust the Spirit, and never look back.

IT'S TIME TO CLAIM YOUR EXCESS BAGGAGE AND THROW IT OVERBOARD

Farmer Jones was working in his field when the pastor came sauntering by. "That's a mighty fine field of corn the Lord has given you," said the pastor piously.

"Well," said the farmer sweating profusely, "you should've seen it when the Lord was working it all by himself!"

✝

To each of us has been entrusted for a time a small piece of this earth to bring to life and to flower. It's the great journey of our life, so we need to hear what Jesus said of it so long ago. "Travel light," he said. "Your journey will test every fiber of your soul and at times success will seem utterly beyond your reach. Travel light!"

We all carry excess baggage, much of it in our heads. For some of us it's fear. For some it's shopworn ideas that have long passed their "sell by" date. For some, it's a compulsive need to win and to possess.

Whatever our baggage, it keeps us frozen in a state of spiritual infancy. We believe the seductive inner voice that whispers, "You *have* to be rich, you *have* to prevail, you *have* to keep up pretenses, or you won't be you." It promises safety and security but delivers nothing but a dusty field devoid of life.

✝

Give your heart to the hopes and loves that are true. And let go of all the rest. It won't be easy, because your baggage feels like a part of you. But the Spirit, who is God's strength, will touch you in your weakness and draw you forward step by step. You'll complete your great journey. And your small piece of the earth will come to life and flower!

IN JESUS' HEART, THERE'S ALWAYS ROOM FOR ONE MORE

A man was already late as the subway doors closed and he spotted one of his new leather gloves lying on the platform. He couldn't get out to retrieve it, and there was no one to hand it up. So in a flash he grabbed the other glove and tossed *it* onto the platform too. "At least someone's going to have a good pair of gloves," he thought to himself. And he began to smile.

†

It was a small matter, over in seconds, but it spoke volumes about his soul. He'd been irate for a moment, but then let go of the anger and transformed his loss into someone else's gain. It wasn't an accident, but a habit rooted in years of thinking beyond the confines of his own skin.

It's so easy to get marooned inside ourselves, so immersed in our wants and hurts that we live as if we're the only ones who count. It's called self-absorption, and it should frighten us, for it can render us immune to love and friendship - even with God.

Jesus' good Samaritan story is his plea for us to re-define our family tree and to make a place in it for all his people: no more Insiders vs Outsiders, just a huge circle with room for everyone. Living that way isn't easy, because our hearts seem to have automatic door closers that work when we're not looking. The answer, as Jesus said so often, is to stay awake. When we find our hearts turning to stone and our hands filling with stones, we'll remember how helpless *we'd* be if God weren't so full of second chances.

†

If you want loves that last and joys that fill your soul, build a heart like Jesus' heart, where there's always room for one more. It will cost you terribly at times, as it cost Jesus. But it's the only road to the peace we all long for.

HAS *YOUR* HEART GONE AWOL?

Mom had guests for dinner and asked little Annie to say grace.

The child blushed: "I don't know what to say when company's here."

"Just say what you've heard me say," said mom.

So Annie bowed her head and this is what she said: "Oh Lord, what was I thinking when I invited all these people to dinner? Amen."

✝

Hospitality is tricky. There's a lot more to it than pouring a good wine and grilling a rare steak. It's about the heart, which Jesus' old friend Martha had yet to understand. She was rushing about trying to make everything just right. But all the while, her head was filled with silent screams: "Why doesn't that lazy sister of mine lend a hand? I just know Jesus is going to hate the lamb! Why did he have to bring those scruffy apostles? Maybe they'll leave early!"

Like Martha we often forget that the main purpose of life isn't just about getting things done. After all, Hitler built the autobahn and Mussolini made the trains run on time. Life's real purpose is communion: being family for one another. Our time on earth isn't about earning enough brownie points to get into heaven. It's about becoming the family we're going to *be* forever.

Jesus showed us the way. He brought a listening heart to everyone He met and made Himself so completely present that each one felt specially chosen and drawn into the circle of His love. His love was life changing because his heart was fully engaged.

✝

Don't let *your* heart go AWOL! Walk with Jesus and learn how to build a welcoming heart with room in it for all of God's people. Step by step, you'll find your way to the joy and peace of God's family which will be your home for all eternity.

YOU CAN TRUST OUR FATHER
WITH YOUR LIFE

A notice was posted in a hospital's staff lounge: "Remember, the first five minutes of life are the most dangerous." Underneath, someone had scribbled: "The last five are pretty risky too."

✝

And as for that, the time in between is no cakewalk! Every day we see tragedies that take our breath away: the little girl who gets AIDS from a transfusion, the marine who comes home with no legs, the retired couple thrust into poverty for the rest of their "golden years." We say to ourselves: "I could never handle that!" And we'd be right, for a *lifetime of hurt is more than anyone can endure all in one piece.*

But we have an alternative. God has hidden remarkable gifts and strengths within our reach. And as each day unfolds, he can help us find what we need for the day, if we're listening. He did it for the ancient Israelites as they wandered in the desert, lost, hungry and despairing. Each morning they found manna waiting for them. It came every morning, always just enough, year after year, until the day they reached the Promised Land and didn't need it any more.

And so it will be with us, if we trust the Lord enough to take life one day at a time, confident that tomorrow he'll again help us to find what we need for that day. Our troubles won't disappear, but they'll lose their power to overwhelm us.

When Jesus gave us the Our Father, he was showing us how we ought to pray. It's not a prayer of anxious pleading, but the calm prayer of people who know their Father can be trusted. It's supremely confident in its last line, "Lead us not into temptation," or a more accurate translation, *"Bring us not to the breaking point."* Those who *know* our Father have no such fears.

✝

Jesus' special name for God was Abba - Papa. Trust him and walk with him confidently, one day at a time. You will eventually die, but he'll never let you be destroyed. Take his hand and never be afraid again.

Ordinary 18 - C
Luke 12:13-21

HAVE YOU BEEN LED ASTRAY BY YOUR STUFF?

A couple stopped for lunch at a town whose unpronounceable name led to an argument. When they reached the fast-food window, the wife asked for help: "Sir, before you take our order, would you *please* pronounce the name of this place...very slowly."

"Sure," said the young man: "BURRR...GERRR...KING."

†

So much of what we say and do makes little sense. Lest we forget that, Jesus told a story about a rich man who was blessed with a harvest sufficient for ten lifetimes. Apparently he thought he was going to live that long, because he ordered huge barns to store it all. But the barns were never built, for that very night he died and his "harvest of the century" was left to the birds and the mice.

In a world of ceaseless change, concrete things are comforting. We can see them, touch them, get a deed to them, put them in a safe. They give us the illusion of having *something* we can count on. So we go after more and more and find that our very identity is starting to depend on *more*. That's not the life God wants for us.

Think about the persons you most admire. There's something special about them, a largeness of soul, an inner calm, a gladness of heart even on the hard days. They're not anxious about losing, because their life isn't about winning and having. They've learned from Jesus that it's about sharing.

Much of life is mystery, and for many of our questions there'll be no answers in this life. But for the ultimate question, "How can I find peace in this unpredictable world?" Jesus gave the answer: "What you have received as a gift, give as a gift."

†

Give what you have, your laughter, your tears, your words, your silence, the fruit of your garden and the work of your hands. But most of all, give your heart. In doing that, you'll grow into Jesus' likeness. And you'll be ready for the eternity you were created to spend with Him and all his family.

KEEP YOUR DAY ON COURSE WITH MOMENTS OF HONEST REMEMBERING

A little girl was showing a classmate around her house. When they got to the bathroom, she said, "Don't step on those scales!"

"Why, what's wrong with them?" asked her friend.

"I don't know, but every time mom steps on them, she screams."

✝

Scales don't lie, but sometimes *we* do. We start small, and then escalate:

- At first: "Mommy, a pixie came and used up all your lipstick."

- Before long: "The check is in the mail."

- And finally, on Good Friday: "I don't know the man!"

Jesus told us, "Where your treasure is, there your heart will be." So what *is* our treasure? Most of us have a pre-recorded answer: my family, my friends, the Lord. But is it true? The patterns of our choices will tell us. How do we treat the folks we *say* are our treasures? Do they get the leftovers of our time and attention? And what does the Lord get from us? A distracted

Hail Mary from time to time? Most of us name what our treasures *ought* to be, but quickly lose focus amidst the busyness of daily life.

We can do something about that by sprinkling moments of honest remembering through the day: "Lord, this day hasn't started well. Please stay close." Or "Lord, Ed needs special attention today. Help me to be there for him." Or "Lord, what a sunset! Thank-you!"

✝

These tiny moments of remembering can keep you on track and change the tone of your day. Make them a regular part of your life, and *discover* the difference between traveling alone and having a partner for life!

Ordinary 20 - C
Luke 12:49-53

DON'T SETTLE FOR A COVER-UP!

A man walked into a bar and tried to sell his dog.

"I don't need a dog," said the bartender.

But then the dog spoke. "Please, sir, this man is mean; he never takes me for walks; he never feeds me, he coops me up for days."

"Hey," said the barman, "This dog can talk. Why're you selling him?"

"I'll tell you why," growled the owner: "I'm tired of all his lies!"

✝

Our habit of lying to ourselves as well as to others provoked some shocking words from Jesus: "I've come for division, not peace!" He wasn't giving up on love and reconciliation, and he certainly wasn't advocating holy wars. He was telling us that what we call peace is often not peace at all, but just a cover-up, a lie. He was pressing us to embrace the truth and to deal with the very real conflicts within us and around us, instead of pretending they're not there. It's work that needs to be done, but we can't do it alone.

If our marriages, families and communities are to be more than battlegrounds, we have to let the loving wisdom that *is* the Spirit break through our fears and defenses and set us on fire. With that holy fire in our hearts, there's no failure of our own that we cannot face and no neighbor to whom we cannot speak the truth. The truth will set us free, because love has taught us to give it as a gift and not use it as a weapon. By naming in love what divides and diminishes us, we'll lay the foundations for solid bridges that will bring us together in peace.

✝

Let the Spirit set you on fire and create in you the wise and fearless heart of a true bridge builder. There's great work to be done, and the energy for it is within your reach.

BE TRUE AND BE FREE!

The wife of an executive decided to pay her husband a surprise visit. But when she opened his office door, she found a secretary sitting in his lap. Without missing a beat, he continued his dictation: "...and in conclusion, gentlemen, I simply cannot continue to function in this office with just one chair!"

†

At times we're all tempted to re-define reality to fit our own purposes, and some of us are quite adept at persuading ourselves that our version is true. But saying it doesn't make it so, because some ways of living will just never be right, never work in the long run, never bring us peace and content-ment, no matter what eloquent baloney we feed ourselves.

That's what Jesus is telling us when he says, "If you want to save your life, you have to enter by the narrow door." We not only have to *tell* the truth, especially to ourselves. We have to *live* the truth, and *be* true from the inside out. "Be true, be true, be true," were the plaintive last words of *The Scarlet Letter's* Reverend Dimmesdale after decades of living a lie.

Being true and living true isn't easy. It requires facing up to hard things and doing hard things. (That's why Jesus calls it "the *narrow* door.") But it's the only way of living that works in the end. As Jesus said, the truth can set us free, free from illusion and self-deception and free to build lives where the thought of being fully known holds no dread for us.

✝

Enter through the narrow door: Be true, and be free!

IMPERFECT BUT WORTH LOVING

Two old friends were musing about the wisdom that's supposed to come with age. "When I was young," said the one, "I worried constantly about what other people thought of me. As I grew older, I said, 'I don't care what they think.' And now that I'm really old, I realize they aren't thinking about me at all!"

✝

Our desire for the good opinion of others is natural. But it can easily morph into pretensions that we're superior to our neighbors and entitled to special privileges. We can find ourselves echoing the pharisee: "Thank God I'm not like the rest of men!" Sustaining such pretensions is full time work, so much energy spent on *looking* good, *having* the right stuff, and always *being* right. But sooner or later, the lonely Wizard who lurks in every one of us *will* be unmasked.

Why are we so resistant to that moment of truth? The villain is fear. We are wonderfully made, but having to face our repeated mistakes and painful limitations day after day can make us afraid that *we're not much at all.* So we try to hide our feet of clay, treading the ancient path of Adam and Eve and their failed fig leaves.

If only we'd let go of our fears, we'd see ourselves as God sees us, *imperfect but worth loving.* We'd be free at last for our *real* life's work: becoming

full-time members of God's family and embracing every human being as
our brother or sister - no more, no less. *Remember what you
are about, because you are about good things*

✝

Relax in the Lord! *Let* God *be* God. As you allow his love to wrap you
round and warm your soul, your fears will recede and with them all the
wasteful pretensions that cut you off from him and from his people.

HAVE YOU CEASED WONDERING
WITH THE SPIRIT?

We all have childhood memories of asking ourselves over and over, "What will I be when I grow up?" Those were magic moments, so full of possibilities; but for most of us they seem gone forever. That's a shame, because "what am I going to be?" is *not* a one-time question just for children. It should be a daily question for us all, as our lives continue to unfold, with old doors closing and new ones opening.

So how do we retrieve the habit of productive wondering? We begin by opening ourselves to seeing what the Spirit sees. That Spirit-guided probing will set us on the road to startling surprises and serious stretching. For the Spirit blows where it will and is not to be tamed.

The wisdom that beckons us concerns more than just a role or a job, but a way of *being with and for* God's people in *this* time and *this* place - not some former or future place. If we persist in listening to the Spirit and refusing to set narrow limits on what we're willing to hear, our life will grow large and those around us will thrive.

Think of the old granny in her walker. Her husband is dead, her children are long grown, and poor health has forced her into a rest home. Most of her life is behind her, but she still has a life's work. She's the glue that holds a big family together, the wise and kind heart that listens to troubles and wipes away tears. She's their model of quiet hope and silent thankfulness. That's her life's work now, and it surely is worth her life.

For each of us, young or old, weak or strong, there is such a work *now*, rich and many-sided, waiting for our attention and our commitment. Let the Spirit be your guide and your strength. And be not afraid!

Ordinary 24 - C
Luke 18:1-32

WHAT YOU'VE RECEIVED AS A GIFT, GIVE AS A GIFT

It would be hard to find a clearer view into Jesus' soul than the sneering words of his critics: "He welcomes sinners and eats with them!" That was the essence of the man. He didn't just tolerate sinners, he *welcomed* them: "Come on in. You're just in time for supper. Sit here by me!"

Jesus looked into the hearts of the most troubled sinners and found brothers and sisters. He took them into his life and made them glad to be alive. That's the same embrace he's offering us, an extraordinary gift that calls for a response. But *how* to respond?

Jesus said: "What you've received as a gift, give as a gift." Give hope to your faltering brothers and sisters by recognizing the good in them, speaking it aloud, and helping it to grow. What could be more natural? And yet it seems we have to struggle mightily to do it. It's as if we thought a smile or a kind word were non-renewable resources: give too many away and you'll run out!

Our reluctance to welcome and to engage one another wholeheartedly, and without exceptions, is a sickness that needs to be healed. For it will harden our hearts so that we'll never be able to take in the love that *is* Jesus. We'll leave him on the outside of our souls. And we'll remain judges, not lovers.

We can prevent that tragedy if we remember that, contrary to that pomp-ous Pharisee, we're *all* "like the rest of men," flawed and frail, and often not very loveable. And yet the Lord keeps welcoming us anyway. The only response that makes any sense is a response *in kind*, a grateful readiness to welcome everyone inside the circle of our love and to leave no one outside.

"What you've received as a gift, give as a gift!"

ARE YOU TAKING WHAT ISN'T YOURS?

A young man was thrilled with his first apartment. But he confided to his best friend: "there are some weird people upstairs. Every morning around 3 AM they start jumping up and down on the floor."

"Wow," said his friend, "have you complained?"

"No, it's no problem. That's when I practice my trombone."

✝

Jesus was stern in his warnings about cheating others of what's rightly theirs. But most of us write ourselves out of that script: "I'd never cheat a poor person or sell something that's defective. And I can't even spell embezzlement."

Probably true, but in more subtle ways, we *do* cheat our neighbors at times. We cheat them of their self-esteem with our put-downs. We rob them of their good name with our gossip. We take moments that should be happy and turn them ugly. We invade their times of quiet and leave them frag-mented. Such unjust patterns can have no place in our lives. We need to name them, claim them, feel their wrongness, and fix them.

Our first instinct is to make stern resolutions to *eradicate* them, but that generally comes to nothing. Real change requires a positive act: replacing what's wrong with something right. Replace put-downs with patient listening. Replace gossip with affirmation. Replace our intrusive noise with the gift of quiet. Replace bullying with defense of the weak.

Those individual acts will find coherence and energy if we embrace the overall vision of becoming for one another what Jesus always is for us. He's always welcoming, listening, understanding, forgiving, encouraging, patient. And he's always there.

†

As you labor with Jesus' help to build that kind of heart, much of what you've thought important will fall away and be left at the roadside. What truly matters will become clear: life given and received one day at a time, life shared in peace.

HAVE YOU BUILT A COCOON
FOR YOURSELF?

A wife was going away for a few days, so she made a "Honey-Do" list of six items for her husband. Then, just for fun, she added one more:

"#7. Think about your wife a lot."

When she returned, her husband reported proudly that he'd completed everything except #7. "What's this!" she said. "Didn't you think about me while I was gone?"

"I started," he said, "but I just couldn't finish!"

✝

That's the way *we're* supposed to be, carrying in our hearts the people who make up our lives and never letting them slip away. But too often we wander off into a little world all our own. That's why Jesus gave us the story of the rich man who lived in a lavish cocoon he'd made for himself, blind to the needs of the starving man on his doorstep, and deaf to the hopes and hurts of his own family. And then, before he knew it, his life was over. The beggar was nestled in the bosom of Abraham, while *he* was in hell! The deep chasm he'd been digging all his life had cut him off from God and his people. He was entirely alone.

If we want a life that *is* a life, it can't be just about our own convenience and well-being. It has to be about *the whole lot of us,* making a home for one another, with all the demands and inconveniences that implies, and helping one another to thrive. To forget that is to risk a long, tragic retreat to a solitary place, where we'll languish without love for all eternity. God won't send us there. We'll walk there all on our own, muttering as we dig the chasm around us deeper and deeper, "If I just get the right stuff, my life will be perfect."

†

Your life is about *us. Keep* that at the center of your heart. Embrace the challenges it implies. And all else will work for the good.

Ordinary 28- C
Luke 17:1-19

LIVE GRATEFULLY: GIVE YOURSELF AWAY!

Two elderly women met for the first time since graduation. "You were always so organized," said the one. "Have you lived a well planned life?"

"I have," said her friend. "I married a millionaire, then an actor, then a preacher, and finally an undertaker."

"Interesting, but how did that make a well planned life?"

"Simple," she said. "One for the money, two for the show, three to get ready, and four to go."

†

Building a good life takes conscious effort, but even then much of what comes our way is unearned gift. We didn't earn our parents or our native talents or our birth in a free country. It was all gift! But as with most of the lepers that Jesus healed, our gratitude doesn't run very deep. And that leaves our souls impoverished and narrow - we don't see, we don't rejoice.

Thankfulness isn't like paying a bill: *You* do *me* a favor, *I* send *you* a note, and that's the end of it. True thankfulness begins with a dawning awareness that we are known and held dear by the One who gave us life! When we "get" that, our hearts experience a joy we can't keep to ourselves. We *have* to share the life-changing gift of being cherished and understood!

For the grateful soul that discovers that, life ceases to be a dreary routine and becomes instead a joyful unfolding of the great and understanding heart we've always wanted to be.

✝

That's where *living gratefully* can take you. And there's no better place in all the world.

GOD CAN BE TRUSTED WITH *YOUR* LIFE

A mother was walking on the beach with her little girl who spotted a piece of candy and started to pick it up. "Don't touch that!" said mom. "It's full of germs that'll make you sick."

"Mommy," asked the child, "how do you know all these things?"

"They're on the mommy test," she said. "If you don't pass the test, you can't be a mommy."

"Oh, I get it. If you flunk the mommy test, you have to be a daddy!"

✝

Whether you're a mommy *or* a daddy, making a good life is hard work and there's no substitute for *persistence*. That's half of what Jesus tells us about prayer. And the other half is *confidence* that God can be trusted with our lives.

God doesn't need a daily briefing from us, nor does he have to be nagged into helping us; his heart is already there. *We're* the ones whose hearts need to change, and that's what prayer is about. If we approach the Lord with affectionate trust and then don't pull away - as we're so wont to do - our hearts will slowly become more attuned to him. We'll experience subtle shifts in our hopes and aspirations and find ourselves beginning to see the world as he sees it and to want what he wants.

Foolish ideas and ambitions that we've treasured for too long will begin to evaporate as our long-term conversation with the Lord continues. Changes we've labeled "impossible" will get re-labeled as "possible." Hopes we've allowed to die, will come alive again. All of that will happen, if we persist in that heart-to-heart conversation and hold firm to our conviction that God *can* be trusted with our lives.

†

It's a life-and-death truth: our very dear Father *can* be trusted with *your* life! So why not give it to him *now*?

Ordinary 30 - C
Luke 18:9-14

IF YOU WANT PEACE, WORK FOR JUSTICE

A couple was out hiking when they came upon a huge canyon with a sign: *Echo Point*. "Try it," said the wife.

To be a good sport, he shouted, "baloney!" Nothing happened.

"Try it again," she urged.

This time he shouted, "I'm the greatest man in the world."

The echo came back, "baloney!"

†

We all talk a little baloney, most of it innocuous but some of it quite harmful. That's why Jesus gave us the story about the self-absorbed Pharisee. He lived by the rules and stayed out of trouble, but he was blind to his own soul and so was captured by a lie: "Thank God I'm not like the rest of men!" At the core of that delusion is a kind of amnesia. It forgets that, where God is concerned, we're all permanently on welfare, God's version of Aid for Dependent Children.

None of us can say, "I don't need God to understand me and keep me alive." We may not *say* or even *think* it, but we may *live* it, and that does immeasurable harm. For any time we deny our dependence on God, we also deny the common bond between all of "us" and all of "them." We lay the foundations for cruelty and oppression and feel free to turn our backs on most of God's people. That must not be.

If peace is ever to come to our world, it will be grounded in justice that knows there can be no more "us" vs "them," just brothers and sisters who *owe* one another respect and understanding

†

"Brother" and "sister." Speak those words from your heart often and let your every deed match those words. God's kingdom will surely come. If you want peace, work for justice.

HE LOVED YOU EVEN BEFORE
HE MADE YOU

A parishioner came to visit his elderly pastor who was dying. "Would you like me to read to you, Father?" he asked.

"Oh yes!" said the priest. "The book of Chronicles, chapter one."

It was a tough read, a genealogy with 54 verses of unpronounceable names: Methusaleh, Jehosephat, Arpaschad, Almodad, and on and on. But the old man listened with rapt attention, and when it was done he smiled: "How comforting. Just think, God knew them all by name."

✝

Have you ever wondered if God has forgotten you or regrets having made you? It's a troubling question, but our own life experience suggests an answer. When a baby is born, its parents know what lies ahead: dirty diapers, sleepless nights, measles, mumps, chicken pox, oceans of tears, adolescence, driver's license. Yet those parents welcome their baby because, even before it's born they've invested their hearts in it.

And so it is with God and *his* children. But sometimes the humiliating record of our repeated sins and mistakes can weigh so heavily upon us that we imagine God being as disgusted with us as we are with ourselves. When we do that, we're not seeing reality. We're projecting our *own* smallness onto God. But God *isn't* small and he doesn't *think* small! The ultimate proof of that is the risen Jesus, God *with* us, God *for* us, always.

†

Look into the face of Jesus on the cross, the understanding face of love without limits. Let your heart rejoice. And never doubt the depth of God's hopes for you, the loving hopes of our very dear father, who will never turn away.

ARE YOU TRAPPED INSIDE YOURSELF?

A wealthy society matron went to a psychiatrist who made a seemingly innocent request: "Tell me about yourself." She complied with delight: three times a week for nearly a year! When her weary doctor finally managed to break through her monologue, his advice was blunt: "Take the first train to Niagara Falls and take a good long look at something bigger than yourself!"

†

Self-absorption is an ugly habit and none of us is immune, not the young who're fixated on *their* pals, *their* pimples, and having *their* way, nor the old who're fixated on *their* heartburn, *their* certitudes, and having *their* way, nor those in the middle who're fixated on *their* careers, *their* Chardonnay, and *having their* way.

Young or old, we all have our obsessions and delusions that let us think we're the center of the universe and the only ones who really count. For awhile we may succeed in evading the hard truth that by ourselves we're no more than fly specks. But eventually reality will break through and we'll find ourselves empty and alone, terrified of dying and seeing no future.

It's a dismal prospect, but not inevitable. Jesus invested his whole life in showing the alternative. It begins with a great leap *beyond* ourselves: reaching for Jesus' hand, and then with his help, taking our neighbors' hands and giving ourselves away without counting the cost. Our mortality won't terrify us anymore, because there'll be more to us than just *us*: the Lord and his people will be our center, our comfort, and our sure and certain hope!

†

Put down deep roots in the Lord and his people. Become a first-class listener and learn how to hear the cries of those who need you. Your whole life will change, and the people around you will be the first to notice!

WHAT KIND OF HEART ARE YOU MAKING?

For many centuries, fierce Old Testament readings have been used by preachers as the theological equivalent of "just wait till your father gets home!" It was a strategy for scaring people into being good, and we could say it worked, if we define goodness as just staying out of trouble. But frightened obedience to an *imagined* despot can never bring us to the *real* God or create kind hearts within us.

What will it be like to die and come before the *real* God? Will a ledger of all our deeds be read and then a judgment rendered? That won't be necessary, for our heart *is* our ledger, the composite of all our choices across a lifetime. And it will speak for itself.

Not even the best of us will be perfectly ready to step into our father's embrace. But he has no intention of losing us. Somehow, he'll help us to finish up. That's the real meaning of purgatory, not a place of pointless punishment, but a state of final healing for those whose hearts are open to his touch.

If there's an element of fear in dying, it shouldn't be about God, whose love never falters. It should be about the hearts we've been making. At our very center, is there a family resemblance between us and our brother Jesus? An honest answer is that we all need something of a remake, and we'd better get to it while there's time.

LIFE'S TROUBLES AREN'T ABOUT PUNISHMENT. THEY'RE ABOUT GROWING WHOLE!

A woman was puzzled by a verse from the prophet *Malachi:* "The Lord will sit refining and purifying silver." So she visited a silversmith and watched as he held a piece of silver where the flame was hottest to burn out all the impurities. "That's what life's troubles can do for our souls," she thought to herself, "if we don't run away."

"But how do you know when the silver is fully refined?" she asked the silversmith.

"I just wait" he said, "until I can see my face in it."

✝

We were made for happiness. But if we're ever to find it, we must build hearts so spacious and welcoming that they slowly let the face of Jesus shine through. That's a tall order, for we're habitually forgetful and prone to lose our way even on the clearest of days.

But God doesn't abandon us to aimless wandering. He's embedded in his creation many ways of keeping us searching until we understand the roots of our discontent. Like the silversmith, he allows our feet to be "put to the fire," but it isn't about punishment. The challenges and hardships, which are a natural part of life, are God's way of pressing us to examine our values and our conduct and to let go of whatever is shrinking our hearts. If we "go with God" at such moments and don't falter in mid-course, what's broken in us will begin to heal and the growth of our hearts will be one of life's great surprises.

✝

When troubles come, don't flee them. Let them change you, however long it takes. When you're done, the face you'll see in the mirror will be different. It will still be yours, but in a lovely way, it will be Jesus' face as well, and it will be wearing a smile!

✝

Let no day end without asking: what kind of heart was I making today? What kind of heart am I bringing to the Lord? Face the truth and don't be afraid. Our Father will be with you at every step, and his fondest desire is to see you truly whole and safely home.

Rest in the Holy Spirit

Made in the USA
San Bernardino, CA
10 January 2015